THE WORLD OF

MARATHONS

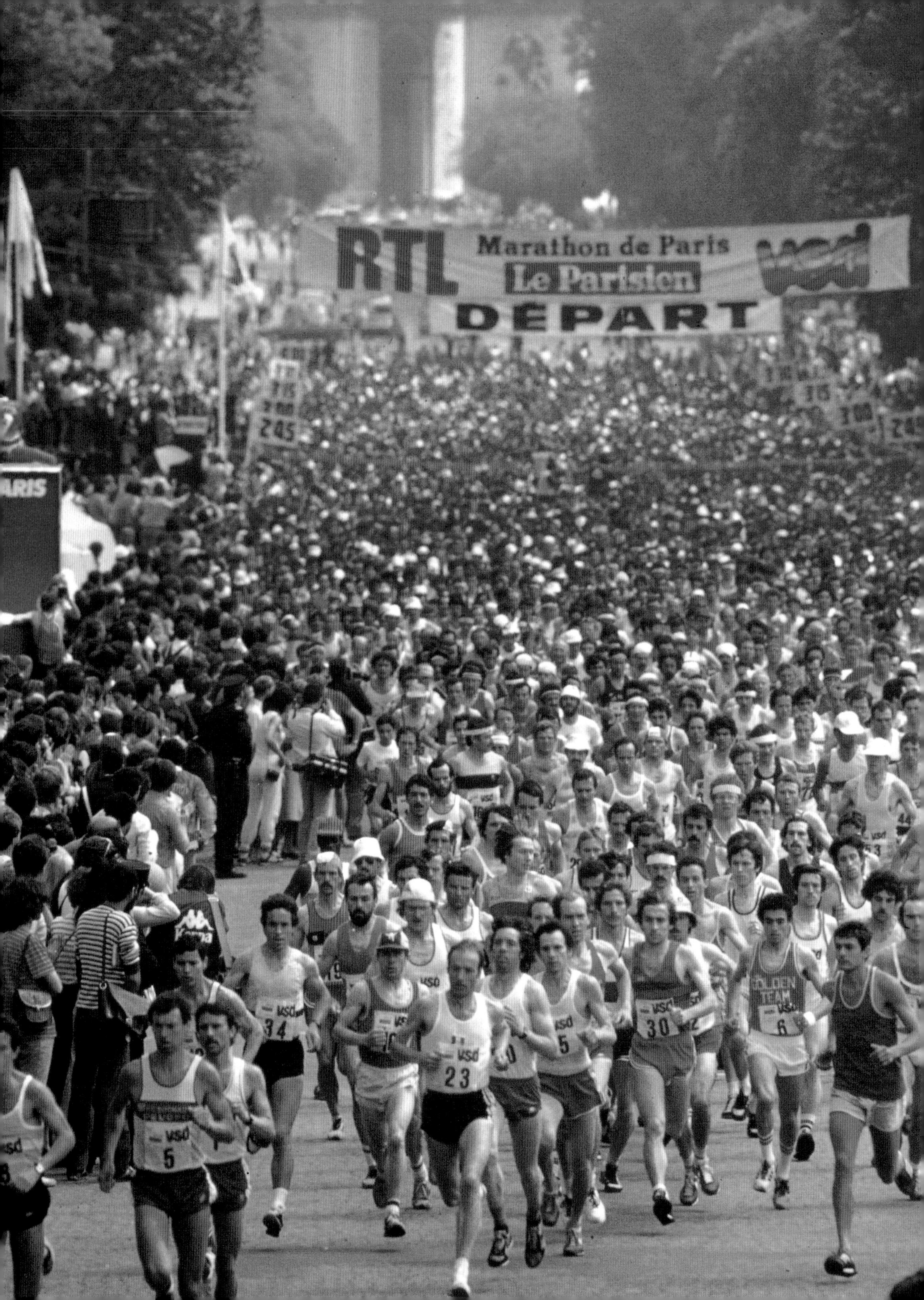
RTL
Marathon de Paris
Le Parisien
DÉPART

THE WORLD OF
MARATHONS

SANDY TREADWELL

FOREWORD
BY FRED LEBOW

STEWART, TABORI & CHANG

NEW YORK

Page 1, clockwise from top left: Bill Rodgers finishes the 1981 Boston Marathon; Rio's marathoners in Flamengo Park; legs along The Mall in London; Grete Waitz wins her sixth New York City Marathon.
Frontispiece: The start of the 1982 Paris Marathon on Avenue Foch.
Title page: The author in the 1982 London Marathon.

Design: J. C. Suarès

      Virginia Pope

Maps: George Colbert

Copyright © 1987 Sandy Treadwell.

Credits for all photographs appear on page 192.

87 88 89 90 91 9 8 7 6 5 4 3 2 1

Library of Congress cataloging-in-publication data

Treadwell, Sandy.
  The world of marathons.

  1. Marathon running. 2. Running races—History.
3. Marathon running—Records. I. Title.
GV1065.T77 1987   796.4′26   86–23067

ISBN 0-941434-98-2

Published in 1987 by Stewart, Tabori & Chang, Inc.,
740 Broadway, New York, NY 10003
Distributed by Workman Publishing, 1 West 39th Street,
New York, NY 10018

Printed in Japan

Statistics in this book are current as of November 2, 1986.

To Libby, Carrie, and Zach, who were missed each step of the way.

Acknowledgments
I would like to express my gratitude to:
Designer J. C. Suarès and photographer Neil Leifer, whose talents are not only displayed between these covers, but who believed this book was a good idea and made it happen.

  Maureen Graney and Amla Sanghvi of Stewart, Tabori & Chang for their careful editing of words and pictures.

  Tom Gilligan of Marathon Tours for helping to show the way and then getting me there.

  Les Woodcock of Edit Aids, Dr. David Martin of the Association of International Marathons and The Athletics Congress, and Mimi Fahnestock and Gloria Averbuch of the New York Road Runners Club for their invaluable contributions to The Finish.

  The race directors and race founders for generously giving their time during the busiest weeks of their year, most especially Fred Lebow, who also contributed the foreword.

  And Libby Treadwell for everything.

The following publishers have granted permission to quote from copyrighted works:

  On page 9, the Emil Zatopek quote is from *The Marathon: The Runners and the Race* by Norman Giller. Copyright © 1983 Norman Giller. Reprinted by permission of Book Sales Inc.

  On page 16, the Jim Fixx quote is from *The Complete Book of Running* by James F. Fixx. Copyright © 1977 James F. Fixx. Reprinted by permission of Random House Inc.

  On page 20, the Fred Lebow quote is from *Inside the World of Big-Time Marathoning* by Fred Lebow with Richard Woodley. Copyright © 1984 Fred Lebow and Richard Woodley. Reprinted by permission of Rawson Associates.

  On page 21, the Joan Benoit Samuelson quote is from "Her Life is in Apple Pie Order" by Kenny Moore, *Sports Illustrated*, March 4, 1985. Copyright © 1985 Time Inc. Reprinted courtesy of *Sports Illustrated*.

  On page 23, the Grete Waitz quote is from *World Class* by Grete Waitz and Gloria Averbuch. Copyright © 1986 Grete Waitz and Gloria Averbuch. Reprinted by permission of Warner Books.

  On page 120, the Jim Fixx quote is copyright © 1984 The New York Times Company. Reprinted by permission.

CONTENTS

Being both a runner and an author, it was indeed an honor to be asked to contribute to this book. Whenever asked to write, give a lecture, or make a presentation, I become reflective about the sport of running and realize how much the sport has truly progressed.

This book contains written and photographic descriptions of twenty-six major marathons as seen through the eyes of a middle-of-the-pack runner. Speaking from my experiences as both a race director and a mid-level runner, I feel safe in stressing that it is the people well off the pace who lend that "special feeling" to a marathon; they are the ones who inspire, motivate, and excite fellow runners, race directors, and spectators alike. These people are the true "moving force" behind any race.

When I started running in 1969, my sole intent was to improve my tennis game. I never foresaw the day when I would actually run in a marathon. But I think that such an introduction to running is quite typical. The running trend so prevalent around the world today—especially among women—began when many people turned to running for secondary reasons, like I did. They took up running to shed a few pounds, to improve their strength for other sports, or for the benefit of their general health. Eventually, they found that they really enjoyed running for its own sake. Much to their satisfaction and surprise they (and I) found that running presented them with daily challenges, and that they were able to derive a unique feeling of pride and enjoyment from the activity. Hence, we have witnessed the transformation of such people into runners; the record-shattering growth of the sport as the acorn literally raced to develop into the proverbial oak tree.

Several landmark occurrences can be attributed entirely to this recent growth and popularity of running. Notable events that immediately come to mind include: record-setting marathon times for both male and female runners; allowance of women competitors into the Boston Marathon; addition of a women's marathon to the Olympic Games schedule of events; establishment of women-only races all over the world; and, most recently, both the public disclosure of the fact that prize money was given to top marathon winners and the sudden increase in the number of races that actually award prize money.

These events, however, are significant primarily in the elite "semi-professional" world of marathoning. It is important to remember that this sport owes much of its current status and success to the ordinary, hard-working runner.

Can this be proven? Yes. Merely go to First Avenue in New York City during the New York City Marathon. Who is the crowd rooting for? Who are the spectators out there to see, support, help, and cheer on? The middle- and back-of-the-packers—the average, everyday runners with whom they identify, and whom they envy and take great pride in, all at the same time.

I hope this book serves as an impetus to all of you who could be participating in marathons but are not, and a celebration for those of you who do run 26.2-mile races. Remember—if I can do it, then all of you can. I am just an average, everyday middle-of-the-packer myself.

FRED LEBOW
PRESIDENT, NEW YORK ROAD RUNNERS CLUB
RACE DIRECTOR, NEW YORK CITY MARATHON

T H E
START

"If you want to run, then run a mile. If you want to experience another life, run a marathon."
EMIL ZATOPEK, OLYMPIC CHAMPION

Before the race come hundreds of training miles, a requirement with its own daily reward: for this runner, it is a tour of the Arizona desert near Scottsdale.

Until not so very long ago the marathon runner was perceived as worse than lonely. Pounding along the asphalt in sneakers, gym shorts, and plain T-shirt, here was someone whose mind was surely hobbled. People ran for reasons: to catch or hit or kick or shoot balls, to score points; running was a means to an endzone. When games were outgrown, the activity was linked to being late; adults ran to make their planes, trains, and appointments. The word itself was featured in negative expressions. People ran around, ran off at the mouth, ran for cover, ran amok, and ran themselves into the ground. No one ran for fun—no one normal, anyway.

Apart from an annual race in Boston, there was nowhere really for the pioneers to go except back to the neighborhood roads where the reception ranged from bemusement to downright hostility. Even the best of them went unrecognized and was frequently asked to explain himself. "Training for the Olympics," Frank Shorter habitually informed motorists who, finding that answer plausible, nodded and rolled the windows back up.

Shorter showed a massive TV audience what he was up to one August evening in 1972. A surprising first into Munich's Olympic Stadium, he won the marathon wearing a boyish grin under his walrus mustache. When he raised his arms in victory, he unknowingly beckoned in the boom.

Running was awarded the gold medal by Americans, who took to the activity in explosive numbers in the late 1970s. In one three-year period runners welled from six million to twenty million. The boom outdistanced faddishness and gathered a second wind. According to a recent

Sprinter Raelene Boyle, Australia's double silver medalist at the 1972 Olympics, starts the 1983 Melbourne Marathon.

A. C. Nielsen survey, thirty-four million Americans run or jog at least once a year. A Gallup poll states that "about one adult American in seven (fourteen percent) is currently jogging regularly" and "all told, adult and teenage joggers cover an estimated twenty-eight million miles each day, or the equivalent of sixty round trips to the moon." An American Sports Data study reveals that there are now 700,000 "serious" runners who consistently train at least 40 miles per week and whose racing schedules include the 26.2-mile marathon distance. Why on earth? The answers have become bountiful. People run to become fit, to lose weight, to feel young, to live long, to stop smoking, to reduce stress, and often to prove something.

Unlike the blurred existence of so much of modern life, the marathon offers a clear, achievable goal. In a few hours, it explores a runner's cowardice and courage and makes him choose sides. No one has put it better than a sixty-four-year-old entrant in the 1981, inaugural London Marathon. Asked why she had decided to undergo the ordeal, she answered, "This is my own little Everest."

Thanks to the success of the New York City Marathon, the event has spread to five hundred annual locations, including the most public and prestigious climes—the great cities of the world. If one must endure the wall, there is solace to being cheered by multitudes lined along Central Park, Ipanema Beach, and Trafalgar Square.

Here is a Walter Mitty fantasy come true, perhaps the marathon's strongest appeal. The majority of us will never hit a groundstroke on Wimbledon's Center Court, swing a bat in Yankee Stadium, drive a lap at the Indianapolis Motor Speedway, play a round at Augusta National, or shoot a basket in Boston Garden. But no matter age, sex, size, or talent, the dream of competing in a major, international marathon is open to everyone. Behind Joan Benoit, Robert de Castella, Steve Jones, Ingrid Kristiansen, Carlos Lopes, Grete Waitz, and dozens of other elite athletes run thousands of neighbors, colleagues, friends, wives, husbands, children, parents, and grandparents—all covering the same ground on the same day.

Lonely and misunderstood no more, the long-distance runner now enjoys the most democratic of sports. This is appropriate. The marathon began in—and takes its name from—a locale in ancient Greece, where democracy itself was launched.

Top: Spiridon Louis, winner of history's first marathon at the Athens Olympic Games of 1896, wore traditional Greek dress at the victory ceremony. Bottom: The 1908 Olympians began at Windsor Castle at the request of Queen Alexandra, who was unaware that she was establishing the marathon's standard distance.

The Legendary Start

Some two centuries before the word "marathon" variously named an office-copy machine, an oil company, and a footrace, it belonged to a village notable mostly for a military upset. On a summer's day in 490 BC, the Athenian army, outnumbered six-to-one, killed 6,400 Persians and sent the rest of the invaders fleeing to their ships. The messenger Pheidippides ran off in another direction, speeding word of the victory across 24 hilly miles to the concerned residents of Athens. He burst into the ruling chamber and shouted, "Rejoice! We conquer!" He then dropped dead.

Apart from the depressing ending, there is one problem with the story—it almost certainly never happened. Herodotus, alive and writing at the time, fails to mention the heroic run in his account of the battle—not the sort of news item, if true, a scribe would keep to himself.

Herodotus does tell of one Pheidippides, a professional courier employed by the Athenians, who was chosen to dash an SOS to Sparta when the Persian fleet landed. Pheidippides managed the 150-mile assignment in forty-eight hours, delivered the request for military support, and returned home with a disheartening reply: the Spartans were busy celebrating the fete of Carnea, and suggested that the Athenians delay their battle until a more convenient time.

A half-century later, Plutarch was the first to write of a messenger who ran to Athens and expired after announcing victory. Plutarch called the hero Eucles, further confusing history. Time, however, cures all that is illogical.

The ancient Greeks never ran farther than three miles to the finish in their Olympia competitions.

A Histrionic Idea

Greek legend was in vogue in nineteenth-century Europe. By then Herodotus' real-life messenger and Plutarch's scene-shifting device had become entwined. French schoolchildren learned of Pheidippides and his doomed run from Marathon. One who remembered the lesson was Michel Breal, who grew up to become a philologist at the Sorbonne and a colleague of Baron Pierre de Coubertin, who shared his interest in ancient ideas.

When de Coubertin decided to revive the Olympic Games, Breal went along to Athens in 1894 to help with the arrangements. He also contributed a suggestion. It would be a nice idea, Breal said, if the Games of 1896 were to include a race commemorating the Pheidippides legend—a 24-mile run from Marathon to Athens. The thought was pretty outlandish, Breal knew.

Pheidippides collapsed and expired after his run from the Plains of Marathon to midtown Athens, a fictionalized episode that covered 24 miles and survived 2,000 years.

The official's helping hand disqualified Dorando Pietri from winning the Olympics, but the Italian confectioner became the 1908 Games' biggest hero and dramatic evidence to generations that the marathon was a dangerous event.

The Greeks had never been inclined to spend their leisure time running long. The ultimate distance event of the original Games (776 BC to 394 AD) was the "doliches"—twenty-four laps around the stadium, about three miles. How would the marathon have been viewed? "The Greeks would have regarded it as a monstrosity," wrote historian H. D. F. Kitto. The Emperor Theodosos felt the same way about the quadrennial competitions in Olympia, which had long degenerated into professional circuses and carnivals by the time the fourth century neared a close. When Theodosos banned the Games, competitive running disappeared for ages.

Breal expected some difficulty convincing Greek Olympic officials to go along with his idea of an epic rerun. The cross-country running craze that had started in England and hopped the Atlantic to the United States had not traveled so successfully to the southeast. A grand gesture would be required to get his race across, Breal decided. He promised to donate a prize, a gold cup.

Breal could have saved himself a few francs, as it happened. A race from Marathon was not only eagerly accepted, it was quickly regarded by the press with patriotic fervor—the one truly local event of the Games. The official program of the first modern Olympiad stated that the marathon was "evidence of the Greek dedication to freedom as a nation, and the sacrifice of the individual to maintain that freedom."

National honor was on the finish line. To assure that a son of the host nation arrived there first, an assortment of goodies were supplied by publicity-conscious merchants. If the winner was a Greek, these prizes would be added to Breal's cup: a ton of chocolate, a barrel of wine, lifetime supplies of tailored clothes and barber-shop shaves, herds of cattle and sheep, and an antique vase given by the principal financier of the Games, Georgious Averoff. A rumor circulated that Averoff also intended to offer the hand of his daughter and a dowery of one million drachmas. A more likely rumor whispered the deaths of three young Greeks in training.

The First Olympic Champion, Part I

At just before 2:00 PM on April 10, 1896, the fifth and final day of the Games, twenty-five runners stood at the starting line by the Battle of Marathon's warrior-tomb. This time the odds were decidedly with the home side; twenty-one of the starters were Greeks. The local competitors had been selected in two trial races over the course, while none of the foreigners had ever run more than twenty miles. The bad news was that three of the visitors—the Australian Edwin Flack, the American Arthur Blake, and the Frenchman Albin Lermusiaux—had been the first finishers of the 1500-meter race, and Flack had also won the 800.

Strung out along Marathon Road were a hundred thousand spectators, some holding wine and bread for the runners. A capacity crowd of 50,000 waited in brand-new Panathinaikon Stadium, hopeful of at last celebrating a Greek victory.

Back at the start, Colonel M. Papadiamantopoulos described the course and then fired his pistol. The runners began the journey to Athens accompanied by their coaches on bicycles, mounted army troops, physicians in a horse-drawn hospital wagon, and couriers who would ride race reports to the stadium.

The early news was grim: All four foreigners, including the Hungarian Gyula Kellner, were in the lead for the first twenty kilometers, half the race. But the next twelve kilometers were entirely uphill, a brutal climb this hot, cloudless afternoon. Blake collapsed near the 23-kilometer point. Kellner, who would finish third, slowed his pace, allowing a twenty-four-year-old local named Spiridon Louis to pass him. A Greek was now in third place, but still far behind. Lermusiaux paid for his lead-pace beyond the village of Karavati. He slumped to the road, was revived by an alcohol rubdown and resumed the race. At 32 kilometers—the summit of the course—he collapsed again.

By the 1980s the long run was perceived to be within reach of everyone, as the mass start of the Paris Marathon attests.

The new leader was Flack, who was also tiring. He was caught by Louis, and the two exchanged the lead. Less than three miles from the finish, Flack suddenly dropped to the ground. Delirious, he punched the spectator who had helped him to his feet. The Australian was loaded into the hospital wagon. The unknown Louis, who had finished fifth in his trial, ran on to Athens alone.

Colonel Papadiamantopoulos rode into the stadium and announced to the occupants of royal box, "A Greek! A Greek!" More than seven minutes in the lead, a dusty, sweat-soaked figure in a blue-and-white-jersey ran into the stadium's marble entrance. Louis was greeted by the roar of the crowd and the royalty of the country; Prince George and Crown Prince Constantine accompanied him to the finish line. The rest waved handkerchiefs and tiny Greek flags, and tossed straw hats into the air.

Louis became an instant legend. All Greece would hear how he had herded goats across the hills of Maroussi, where he had also been a water-bearer and mail-carrier, an appropriate odd-job for the follower of Pheidippides.

The Race Goes West

Inspired by the Marathon run, Arthur Blake and his fellow Boston Athletic Association members of the US Olympic Team left Athens with the idea of organizing their own race back home. They took their time. The following Patriot's Day—seven months after John J. McDermott's time of 3:25:55.6 had won a marathon of twenty-five miles during a track-and-field meeting in New York—fifteen men assembled at Metcalf's Mill in Ashland, Massachusetts, to run 24.5 miles northeast to the Irvington Street Oval in downtown Boston. New Yorker McDermott won this one too, in 2:55:10. Forced to walk three times, he was also the first to suffer from the Newton Hills.

Boston would become the oldest annual marathon in the world and one of the two most prestigious (Fukuoka, Japan is the other). But at the start, Boston was hardly glamorous. Wrote Jim Fixx in *The Complete Book of Running*, "The course . . . was laid out mainly on dirt roads, and the contestants were mostly local men—machinists, milkmen, farmers—who made their own running shoes, trained without coaching and ran largely on will power."

Among the list of early winners were unknowns who appeared from nowhere. The 1926 race was expected to be won by either the reigning Olympic champion, Finland's Albin Stenroos, or four-time Boston winner Clarence DeMar, a *Boston Herald* typesetter. It was won by John C. Miles, a nineteen-year-old delivery boy from Sydney

Top: Most responsible for gathering the masses to the marathon was the race in New York City, which also bridged the gender gap with world-record runs by Norway's Grete Waitz (F1) in 1978, 1979, and 1980, and Allison Roe (F2) in 1981.

Bottom: Details of the New York City Marathon were adopted by other international races, such as Montreal, which now contains a wheelchair division, a blue line marking the course, and a bridge start.

MARATHONS

Mines, Nova Scotia, who had never run more than ten miles and who wore swimming trunks and white sneakers. Then there was two-time winner Ellison M. "Tarzan" Brown, a Narragansett Indian who first emerged from working the woods of Rhode Island in 1935 dressed in a shirt fashioned from one of his mother's dresses and a pair of torn sneakers which he discarded during the race.

No Boston champion was as unmindful of his image as the remarkable DeMar, winner of seven Bostons between 1911 and 1930 despite a ten-year layoff (1912–1922) caused by the discovery of a heart murmur. Mr. DeMarathon, as he was inevitably nicknamed, also became renowned for his belligerence. During a career that included thirty-three Boston Marathons, he socked a spectator who threw water on his legs, shoved an autograph seeker backwards over a curb, and knocked down several bicyclists. He was known to bruise the egos of reporters as well, snapping post-race interviews shut with "That's a stupid question!"

DeMar was Boston's first major marathon star. He was perceived by the public to be intense, a loner, taciturn, and stoical. These characteristics, it was assumed, must belong as well to others who chose to run so far. These marathoners were eccentrics; maybe even misfits. A fellow would have to be strung out of tune to want to put himself through something so dangerous.

One wall that marathoners are happy to run across is located near Beijing, a city where the running boom is just being heard.

The Candyman Can't

Limp and exhausted, the leader of the 1908 Olympic marathon wobbled into London's White City Stadium. It was obvious to the crowd of 70,000 that Dorando Pietri, a twenty-three-year-old Italian confectioner who had overtaken Charles Hefferon just minutes before, was suddenly in desperate trouble. Pietri turned the wrong way around the track, struggled on for twenty yards, and fell. Responding to the frantic plea of the crowd, he got to his feet and staggered on, this time in the right direction. He fell three more times, each tantalizingly closer to the finish line. Suddenly the American John Hayes arrived in the stadium, and raced around the track. Pietri fell once more, but was caught by British officials who supported him to the finish.

A few hours later, an American protest was upheld. Pietri was disqualified and Hayes, a twenty-two-year-old department-store clerk, was declared the winner. The race nonetheless made Pietri an international hero. He was presented a gold cup by Queen Alexandra in the most popular moment of the Games.

Alexandra was a marathon fan who had requested that the original start of the race be moved back a few hundred yards from downtown Windsor so that the royal family could have better view. The extended course measured 26 miles and 385 yards, or 42.195 kilometers, from the royal lawn of Windsor castle to the royal box at White City.

When the International Amateur Athletic Federation decided at a conference in 1921 to select a standard distance for all marathon races, the 1908 Olympics understandably came to mind.

The event, widely regarded as the most famous marathon ever run, produced another legacy. No matter that the temperature at the start was 78 degrees, that the humidity was high, and that Pietri had doped himself with strychnine, like most of the others in the race. The photograph of Pietri's finish is one of the most famous in sports history. The image of the runner at the tape—eyes hollow, knees buckling, held upright by one official while another was ready to catch him—convinced generations thereafter that the marathon footrace could be a killer even for very fit Olympians.

A wintry training run in London's Richmond Park is a price happily paid for the good fortune of being one of 23,000 selected to start the London Marathon, an event that annually attracts 80,000 applicants.

The Birth of the Mass Marathon

It took nearly seventy years and one misunderstanding to erase the skull-and-crossbones impression from the event; it took the creation of the all-around-the-town New York City Marathon to make people realize that the 26.2-mile distance could be safely and rewardingly run by everyone.

In 1975 Ted Corbitt, a former head of the New York Road Runners Club and a legendary American marathoner, began talking about a marathon for teams from each of the boroughs. That wasn't the way one George Spitz heard it. A community activist and running buff, Spitz excitedly rushed word of Corbitt's five-borough *course* concept to Fred Lebow, the current NYRRC President. Lebow instantly opposed the plan. "It was already difficult enough to put on a marathon in Central Park," he says.

Spitz pressed on, arranging a meeting between Manhattan Borough President Percy Sutton and Lebow. The marathon director presented what he believed were impossible terms—full cooperation of the city and a $20,000 budget. A few days later Sutton announced that the 1976 race would be part of New York's bicentennial celebration, that Mayor Abe Beame guaranteed police protection, and that a sponsor had stepped forward. The Rudin family would donate $25,000 in memory of Samuel Rudin, a real-estate executive, civic leader, philanthropist, and, fifty years before, a long-distance runner.

As a young man Lebow had spent time on the run himself. He fled post-war, Russian-occupied Rumania, and trekked across Europe smuggling sugar and, later, diamonds. In his autobiography, *Inside the World of Big-Time Marathoning*, he writes, "From an early age I was learning about living by your wits, always being on your toes, improvising."

Lebow scrambled once again during the months following his meeting with Sutton. The 1976 New York City Marathon drew 2,000 entrants, four times more than the 1975 race. The astonishing number trampled the budget. With a sprawling, urban happening suddenly and unexpectedly denting his lap, Lebow looked for dollars. Manufacturers Hanover pledged $5,000 in return for printing the bank's name on runners' numbers, and added $3,500 more so that Lebow could rent high-brow Avery Fisher Hall in Lincoln Center for the awards ceremony. Lebow found $5,000 flying about in

The popularity of long distance running began at the end of the Olympic marathon of 1972, when an exuberant Frank Shorter entered Munich's Olympic Stadium, a winning picture that thrilled America.

the foreign but friendly skies of Finnair. Another $5,000 fluttered from the pages of *New Times* magazine. He wound up "taking in about $45,000 and spending about $65,000. But we had our five-borough marathon."

The First Olympic Champion, Part II

Once the New York City Marathon began popularizing big-city marathons for masses of people, all sorts of strange events happened. Network television tuned in live; athletes were allowed to accept over-the-table payments; world records were broken; and women finally achieved Olympic equality.

For the current generation the enduring marathon picture is likely to be the TV image of a slight woman running all alone across the freeways of Los Angeles in grey shorts and singlet with a painter's cap turned back-to-front on her head.

The story of American Joan Benoit's victory in the 1984 Olympic marathon contains legendary stuff: A first-place finish in the US Olympic trial marathon only seventeen days after a knee operation; a bold move three months later, when she surged past the mile-three water station and left the rest of the Olympic field behind; the courage to push herself all the way in the heat, building her lead over World Champion Grete Waitz of Norway to a minute and a half; and a crazy thought at the end.

"Before going into that tunnel (in the Los Angeles Memorial Coliseum), I somehow heard or sensed the crowd inside come to its feet," Benoit told Kenny Moore of *Sports Illustrated.* "I thought, 'This is a dream. This is the first women's Olympic marathon. This could really change my life. It's still not too late. I can hide in here and not come out the other side.'" Instead, the twenty-seven-year-old from Freeport, Maine, ran into view, snatched the cap off her head, raised her arms overhead, and won the gold medal.

"With half the world watching, Joan helped to change the perception of woman," says Katherine Switzer, who first brought worldwide attention to women marathoners when a BAA official unsuccessfully tried to pull her out of the 1967 Boston Marathon. "Joan's sheer bravery and go-for-it attitude was something everyone could relate to. Her run was an enormous social statement."

A Greek ghost was perhaps applauding as well. Not Pheidippides or Spiridon Louis, but a woman named Melpomene who was denied a place in the Olympic starting field of 1896. The week before the race she ran the course accompanied only by cyclists, and unofficially finished in four-and-a-half hours, way ahead of her time.

T H E
COURSE

"An almost deafening cheering went on for miles. I had never experienced anything like it. I was really flying."
GRETE WAITZ, WORLD CHAMPION

Only a kilometer from the finish line in Olympic Stadium but not quite halfway into the race, Stockholm's marathoners complete their first lap of the city on Odengatan.

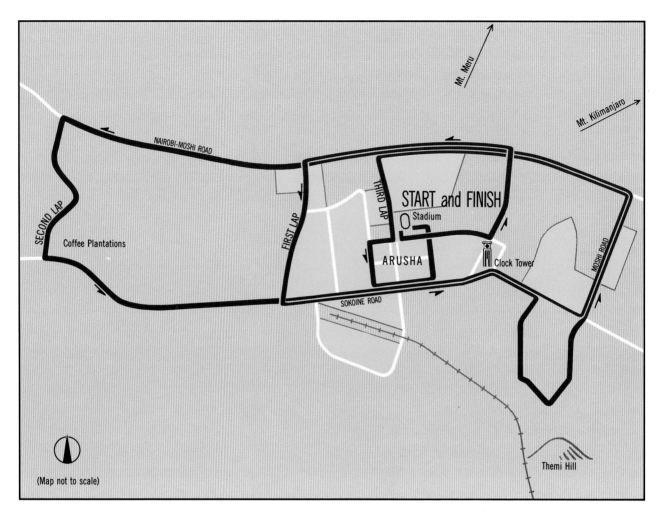

Mount Meru Marathon

ORGANIZER *Mount Meru Marathon*
Post Office Box 855
Arusha
Tanzania
RACE DIRECTOR Ahmed Shariff
DATE Second Sunday in March.
START 8:30 AM in Sheikh Amri Abeid
Stadium.
FINISH Sheikh Amri Abeid Stadium.
TIME LIMIT None.
ELIGIBILITY Open to runners of all abilities; runners must be eighteen years old
by raceday.

AWARDS Trips to the Stockholm Marathon
for top two Tanzanian finishers. Awards to
first twelve male finishers and first five
female finishers. Olympic pins and handicrafts to all foreign finishers. Official
certificate awarded to each finisher.

COURSE RECORDS John Bura, Tanzania,
2:17:49 (1985); Ruth T. Gatti, Tanzania,
3:32:59 (1985).

TEMPERATURE 75°F (24°C)
CROWD 20,000
TERRAIN Three hilly laps, the longest
single climb (10 K to 20 K along the
base of Mt. Meru) mostly during lap two.
COMPETITORS 120 from four nations.
REFRESHMENTS AND SERVICES Water and
cola every 5 kilometers; juice and cola at
the finish.

ENTERTAINMENT Military band at start
and finish.
ADDITIONAL EVENT Awards ceremony.
UNUSUAL FEATURE All foreign entrants
are introduced at the pre-race press conference.

ARUSHA, TANZANIA

MOUNT MERU MARATHON

I sak Dinesen called the Masai tribesmen "noble wanderers." Nothing of this nobility has been lost in the fifty years since her book *Out of Africa* was first published. Lean and graceful, they still walk the plains alone, chins confidently thrust forward as though plowing a path for the rest of the body. They wear brightly colored cloth, decorate their ears with wooden jewelry, and continue to follow Nature's clock, measuring the days by the sun and the seasons by the rains. Wealth is determined by the quantity of goats and cows possessed. As in Dinesen's time, the Masai are disarmed by law in Tanzania and Kenya. In place of spears they carry impotent, blunt poles. Even so, they remain a powerful, exotic presence—timeless sailors on grassy seas.

In March of 1986, an international marathon was dropped among the Masai of Arusha, Tanzania. The Masai stood by the roadside and watched as 112 Tanzanians, two Swedes, two Americans, and an Englishman ran past their mud-and-straw villages. The runners did not appear to be frightened. Nothing dangerous seemed to be chasing them, yet they still scurried uphill in the heat. Eventually, word was passed along that this was a race—three laps around Arusha for no sensible reward. The winner would receive nothing of value, not even a chicken. Then the laughter began.

The bridge leading into the village of Ngaranarok remains open to a variety of traffic on raceday.

First-time marathoner Kathy Jahnige, an American who works in Arusha organizing health projects for the Anglican Church, understood the crowd. "The laughing was very good-natured, I thought," she said. "The thing that was neatest was that even though people didn't understand why I would do such a thing, they still tried hard to help me out. I kept hearing shouts of *'Kazana!'* (Keep going!), *'Jitahidi!'* (Exert yourself!), and *'Pole!'* (Hey, sister!). When I got to the banana trees (mile 18), two women charged me. I thought I was going to get a scolding for showing my legs. But all they wanted was to run alongside, which they did for awhile. It was so sweet."

A few miles earlier, Jahnige had found herself all alone on a stretch of road that divided Arusha's richest coffee plantations. Some of the roadside trees bloomed with crimson flowers. Beyond the rows of ever-green coffee bushes, she could see the peak of Mount Meru above the clouds. If the horizon had been clear, the square, snow-capped summit of Kilimanjaro also would have been visible. The view was spectacular enough, without Africa's highest mountain, to cause Jahnige—whose only goal was to finish the race—to stop and enjoy it. "I felt suddenly like I was in a Rousseau painting," she said.

Henri Rousseau's lions may have been missing from this scene, but they were not far away. The Serengeti National Park, site of the largest migratory concentration of plains game on earth, the Ngorongoro Crater, where lions rule the lush 12½-mile floor of one of the world's natural wonders, and Lake Manyara National Park, famous for the spectacle of prides hanging out on the limbs of acacia trees, are all a half-day's drive from Arusha. Kilimanjaro is even closer. Assisted by a guide and porters, the reasonably fit visitor can accomplish a round-trip climb in five days.

But one Sunday morning in March is all one needs for Tanzania's newest outdoor adventure, Arusha's Mount Meru Marathon. The race arrived from Sweden via Sport-Aid, properly known as the Sports for All Project. Apart from providing equipment and conducting coaching clinics, in three years SFA organized six hundred athletic clubs in the Arusha region, five jogging clubs in the town of Arusha (population 120,000), and the first mass marathon south of the Sahara. (A second has since begun in Dakar, Senegal.)

Half of the marathon's $30,000 budget was funded by Tanzania's national lottery. The Arusha Rotary Club collected a hundred local sponsors, counting the three daughters of a movie-theater owner who donated their allowances. There wasn't money enough for digital clocks on the course and computer timing at the finish. The spirit of the event, though, was on a grand scale, even the courtesy of

Some sixty lions rule the floor of wondrous Ngorongoro, the world's largest intact crater and one of six National Parks surrounding Arusha.

inviting all foreign entrants—including Jahnige—to the pre-race press conference. "You shouldn't measure this marathon by the usual yardmarker," advised SFA Director Jan Frisk.

Also at the press conference was special guest Army Major Juma Ikangaa, Tanzania's own world-class marathoner. Said Ikangaa, "For Tanzania and Africa this race is unique. I hope it will build interest in distance running among younger generations of Tanzanians. Instead of only twelve serious marathoners—the members of the national team—I think there could someday be a few hundred."

The next day three Masai dressed themselves in sky-blue singlets and blood-red shorts and took a run at the future.

The most beautiful section of the exotic course is the hedged road between the coffee plantations west of town, where even the trees are in bloom.

Overleaf: Assembled at the start in 1986 were runners from seventeen of Tanzania's twenty-three regions, many of whom had earned the trip by winning local half-marathons.

ATHENS, GREECE

INTERNATIONAL ATHENS PEACE MARATHON

If Pheidippides could see what has become of the old route from the Plains of Marathon to downtown Athens, he would no doubt die at the sight of the hills, heat, air, and politics.

The International Athens Peace Marathon is the most difficult big-city marathon in the world. The course rises 750 feet in 80-degree temperatures and then plunges into the worst pollution in Europe. "Apart from strangling on the exhaust of 15,000 taxis, the ups and downs will kill you," says George Courmouzis, president of Mondial Tours, who survived from 1978 to 1982 as race director. "I don't know any planner who would choose this place for a roadrace."

The blame sets squarely on history. The course tracks the footprints of two legendary Greeks. The first was the ill-fated messenger who started it all in 490 BC when he rushed home with news of an Athenian victory over the invading Persians. Upon delivering the tidings, he expired on a hillside across from the Acropolis, an act that eventually inspired epic athletic competition. In 1896, during the inaugural modern Olympic Games, a shepherd named Spiridon Louis ran fastest from the ancient battle's warrior-tomb to the new Panathinaikon Stadium in Athens. An instant celebrity of Homeric dimension, his picture was placed in homes, stores, and

Olive branches were presented to the marathoners at the 1982 European Championships.

public squares throughout Greece.

These days, the race honors another hero—and this is where the politics comes in. Tagged onto the race's name and sculpted on the medal is Gregory Lambrakis, a gifted middle-distance runner and politician whose assassination in 1963 was depicted in the movie *Z*. Lambrakis was a communist, a sensitive point as far as the US Embassy and NATO are concerned. "A lot of NATO personnel have received instructions to think twice about running," says Courmouzis.

With three hundred NATO soldiers dismissed from the ranks, foreign entries have fallen well below the one thousand level. Political rhetoric, however, is on the rise. Starting times are reshuffled to accommodate not only all the speeches, but also the protest groups wanting to take part. One year, four hundred Greek Nationalists were given a three-hour lead on the rest of the field. The marathon itself is a political statement.

SEGAS (acronym for the Greek Amateur Athletic Federation) uses its event to deplore commercial exploitation of sport. In other words, no sponsors need apply. Other notable negatives are: no entry fee, no age restriction, no prize money, and, in 1985 at least,

Ten kilometers from the start is the comforting village of Nea Makri, where Marathon Road is flat, the scenery is uplifting, and a few spectators are about.

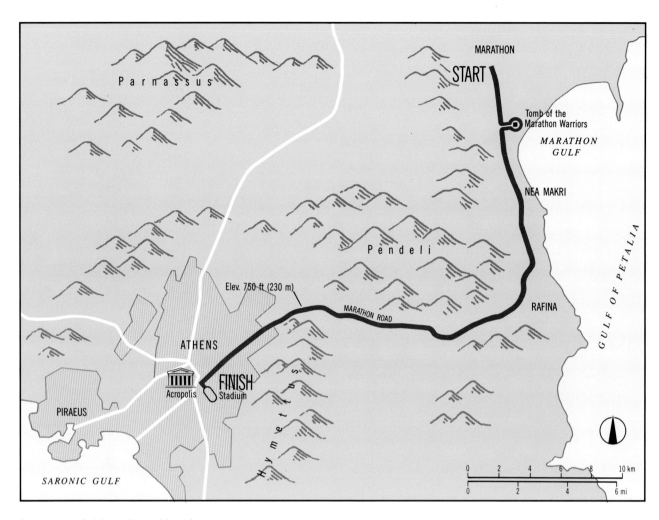

International Athens Peace Marathon

ORGANIZER *SEGAS (Greek Amateur Athletic Federation) 137 Syngrou Street Athens Greece*
RACE DIRECTOR The Board of SEGAS
DATE Second Sunday in October.
START 8:30 AM at Marathon Village.
FINISH Panathinaikon Stadium.
TIME LIMIT Five hours.
ELIGIBILITY Open to runners of all abilities.

AWARDS Awards to top finishers in all age groups. Medals to all finishers. Official certificates awarded to each finisher.
COURSE RECORDS Bill Adcocks, Great Britain, 2:11:07 (1969); Barb Balzer, USA, 2:58:56 (1984).

TEMPERATURE 80°F (27°C)
CROWD 8,000
TERRAIN Mostly flat for the first half, then a 7-mile climb and a 6-mile descent to downtown Athens.
COMPETITORS 1,500 from twenty-seven nations.
REFRESHMENTS AND SERVICES Water and sponges alternating every 2.5 kilometers; post-race cola and juice.

ENTERTAINMENT None.
ADDITIONAL EVENTS Saturday evening pasta party, awards ceremony.
UNUSUAL FEATURES The original run, no corporate sponsorship, no entry fee.

no clocks. The last missing item was the result of a demand from SEGAS that Seiko wipe its name off its faces.

SEGAS is not so picky about other details, however. The first water station is too narrow for the demand placed on it, creating a traffic jam worthy of Athens at rush hour. Farther along the route, the water supply has sometimes run low. So has much of the joy.

When Courmouzis was in charge, three hundred schoolchildren welcomed runners to the towns along Marathon Road with applause, laughter, and a variety of liquids, including Coke, lemonade, and electrolyte drinks. The youngsters of Nea Makri began a tradition of also dispensing olive branches, a classical touch. And at the start, folk dancers performed instead of the current firebrands. But that was a few years ago, before things got heavy and a new SEGAS board of directors banned the travel agent/race director, who they believed was exploiting the event by selling marathon trips to foreigners. His five-year contract was not renewed. SEGAS ignored the obvious irony that tourists had created the annual Athens Marathon.

In 1973, two hundred Finns contacted SEGAS and requested an extended 42.195-kilometer run on the old Olympic course from Marathon Village to the 50,000-capacity marble stadium. The next year the Finns returned, joined by two hundred other vacationers, many of them West Germans. The military crowd soon signed on from area NATO and US Air Force and Navy bases. Courmouzis doubled the civilian count by promoting "The Original Run" to footloose marathoners from twenty-eight countries.

Despite the killing second-half terrain—a seven-mile climb followed by a six-mile descent through fumes guaranteed to yellow T-shirts—ninety percent of the eight hundred remaining foreigners finish Athens. They are joined at the start on the historic battleground by seven hundred Greeks, a third of whom are teenage joy runners who have no chance at all.

Also undaunted by reality is George Courmouzis. He hopes someday to be asked back into his race. Meanwhile, he is trying to establish a marathon around another locale with towering tourist appeal—the pyramids of Egypt.

Despite heat, hills, and pollution, Athens delivers the thrill of following the historic trail from the Plains of Marathon to Panathinaikon Stadium, where Spiridon Louis and the marathon first arrived.

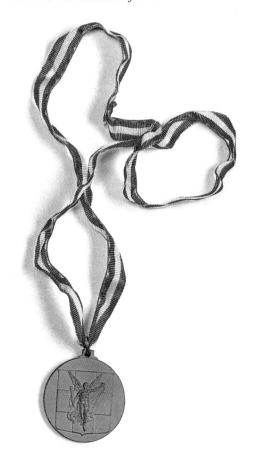

AUCKLAND, NEW ZEALAND

THE WINSTONE MARATHON

No other major marathon is quite like The Winstone Marathon in Auckland, New Zealand. The race is located smack in the drab flatlands of suburbia, 15 miles southeast of the deep blue harbor, tall white skyline, and steep green volcanic hills of the central city. The course, a distorted figure-eight, orbits New Zealand's biggest mall. Starting near a mobile home franchise, the event finishes opposite the mall's Chinese restaurant. At varying points in between are two futuristic cement structures home to the local government and housing authority, a pair of golden arches belonging to McDonald's, a concrete-block factory owned by the sponsor, Winstone Limited, a herd of dairy cows pastured next to a building that mass-produces Big Ben Pies, and a permanent rainbow on the horizon spanning the entrance to Rainbow's End, an amusement park. So much for the local color. (By the way, there isn't a sheep to be found.)

Until a decade ago this was cattle country. Then the city planners, determined to make sense out of Auckland's urban sprawl, moved in. Out went the tractors and in came the bulldozers. From the scraped soil grew something called Manukau City, a rich harvest of fast-food restaurants and light industries. The centerpiece of this

A runner from Owairaka, the event's founding club, grabs the one essential element in marathoning at a station along Kerrs Road.

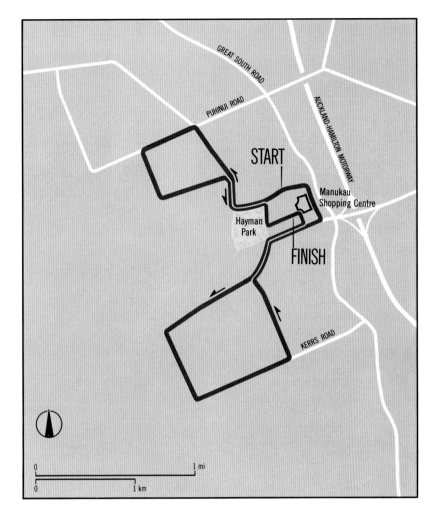

The Winstone Marathon

ORGANIZER *The Winstone Marathon*
Post Office Box 48074
Auckland 7
New Zealand
RACE DIRECTOR Wayne Munro
DATE Third Sunday in November.
START 7:30 AM on Ronwood Avenue.
FINISH Manukau City Centre.
TIME LIMIT None.
ELIGIBILITY Open to runners of all abilities.

AWARDS Awards to top finishers in all age groups, also awards to top teams and local runners. Official certificate and results newspaper mailed to each finisher.
COURSE RECORDS Phil Coppess, USA, 2:11:32 (1985); Yuko Gordon, Hong Kong, 2:41:53 (1984).

TEMPERATURE 60°F (15°C)

CROWD 1,500
TERRAIN Undulating with a 400-meter hill on Wiri Station Road (8, 18½, 29, 39½ kilometers) and a 75-meter rise on Davies Avenue (4, 14½, 25, 35½ kilometers).
COMPETITORS 3,000 from five nations.
REFRESHMENTS AND SERVICES Three stations per lap, each with water, electrolyte drink, and sponges, and none more than 4 kilometers apart; post-race fruit, electrolyte drink, coffee, tea, sponges, massages.

ENTERTAINMENT Two bands along the way, brass band at the finish.
ADDITIONAL EVENTS Ten-kilometer race over one lap of the course just before the marathon, awards ceremony.
UNUSUAL FEATURE All the comings and goings.

satellite community was the mustard-brown Manukau City Shopping Centre, which offered the 200,000 spanking-new residents of Manukau City most anything they might require, including knowledge—the Manukau City Public Library occupies floorspace on the mall's mezzanine.

A progressive thinker named Arthur Lydiard, the legendary running coach and popularizer of long, slow, distance training, settled on Manukau City as a suitable locale for another New Zealand innovation, a people's marathon. He had just returned home to Auckland from a lecture tour of the United States, where he had had a firsthand experience of how the "masses" took to the 1979 Mayor Daley Marathon in Chicago. Manukau City was ideal for such an event, he reasoned. Not only was the terrain as level as one could find on the North Island, other advantages to the site cropped up as well: excellent road surfaces, proximity to Lydiard's own Owairaka Amateur Athletic & Harrier Club, and a promotion-minded city council that would surely be willing to close the course to traffic.

Lydiard had every reason to think big. In the early 1970s, the Lydiard-launched Auckland Joggers Club organized an 11-kilometer race called the Round the Bays Fun Run, which annually attracted

After four laps of the Manukau City Shopping Centre, Winstone finishers are welcomed by a brassy blast from the mall's main entrance.

Right, top: In 1982, New Zealand's Dick Quax lived up to his number-one seeding despite an early challenge from fellowcountryman Trevor Wright and a persistent 25-knot headwind.

Right, bottom: The course is bland from the start, located near a mobile home sales lot, but The Winstone offers its 3,000 travelers a unique atmosphere of camaraderie.

80,000 participants. Having propelled the citizenry into motion, Lydiard believed anything was possible, even a mall marathon. He suggested the event to the club members of Owairaka, asked them to put it on, and took off again for the international lecture circuit.

The job of race director fell to Wayne Munro, an unflappable sports writer and rock critic who once motorcycled the length of Africa with his wife. He now embarked on another mind-bending task, convincing runners that they would enjoy a five-lap race around the Manukau City Shopping Centre. "Initially, the overwhelming opinion was that it would be very, very boring," Munro admits. A field of nine hundred marathoners arrived for the inaugural running nonetheless, and discovered something startling—the race had charm. "Because of the loops, people were running this way and that, constantly passing and encouraging each other," says Munro.

As the years went by, one lap mercifully was eliminated, but the atmosphere never changed. As many as three thousand runners, many of them unofficial, looped the mall each November, cheering themselves around the course and somehow avoiding human gridlock. Munro was content to let the bandits share the road. "We have a policy never to yank a numberless runner," the race director says. "We had seen manhandling scenes spoil too many races. When Arthur gave us this race, we put our heads together and corrected everything we disliked about other marathons."

The Winstone Marathon waits for the last runner to finish before closing down, allows all prizewinners to speak as long as they like at the awards ceremony, gives equal prizes to women, and spreads glory through the ranks. "We even have a survivor's category," Munro says. "You have to have nearly died to qualify. This year's winner had been run over by a truck."

Munro enjoys collecting the human-interest stories of his Winstone entrants. "The best part of this job is that I get to stand at the finish and talk to all these incredible people," he says. "It's a journalist's paradise. Where else could you find a guy who has just carried a 110-pound sack of coal on his back for 42 kilometers?"

The first raceday, Munro was joined by the winner, John Robinson. "He had been touched by all the runners who applauded for him as he lapped them," Munro remembers. "John wanted to applaud the last finisher, who turned out to be a detective named Niwa Kawha." Robinson also bestowed a traditional compliment. "Good on you, mate," he told Kawha. Unlike most other marathons, no one ever thought to give medals to the finishers of The Winstone Marathon. That phrase always seemed reward enough.

Eventual winner Peter Pfitzinger (number 2) led the 1983 field up the 400-meter hill on Wiri Station Road, an obstacle placed within sight of a factory owned by the sponsor, Winstone Limited.

BEIJING, PEOPLE'S REPUBLIC OF CHINA

BEIJING INTERNATIONAL MARATHON

Along with construction cranes on the city skyline, home-appliance ads on the roadside billboards, and English-slogan T-shirts on the trendy youths, hundreds of dawn joggers provide evidence of China's rush toward modernization. Some of the early risers wear shoes made locally in a new Nike factory. Others run in sneakers, or even sandals. All move at a leisurely pace dictated by various practicalities—the air is polluted with coal dust, showers are almost nonexistent, and fitness is the goal, not speed. For the moment, these men and women have no mass race to train for. The single marathon in Beijing is a Japanese import for male athletes only. The masses are required only for the sidelines.

Early on a warm October Sunday, a chunk of the 400,000-person race crowd gathers four-deep along Tienanmen Square. The grand scale of the buildings—the Gate of Heavenly Peace, the Museum of Chinese History, and the Great Hall of the People—minimizes the human presence, except for Chairman Mao. His outsize portrait on the gate's facade dominates this, the heart of China.

The spectators hold multicolored pennants and patiently wait for the reason to wave them. At last, the flashing lights of a police van signal an approaching procession from the eastern end of eight-lane

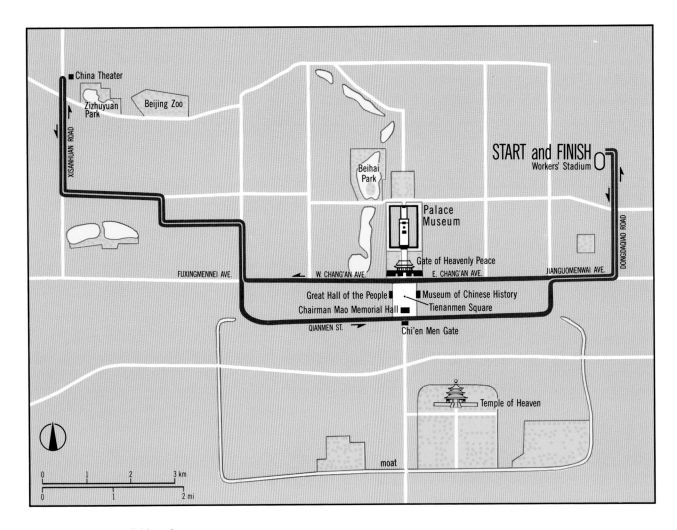

Beijing International Marathon

ORGANIZER *Organizing Committee Beijing International Marathon 9 Tiyuguan Road Beijing China*
RACE DIRECTOR Li Wenyao
DATE A Sunday in October.
START 9:31 AM in Workers' Stadium.
FINISH Workers' Stadium.
TIME LIMIT Runners must reach 25 kilometers in a time of 1:40:00 and 35 kilometers in 2:20:00.
ELIGIBILITY Open to foreign male runners twenty to forty years old who have achieved at least a 2:45:00 marathon time during the previous two years; runners with a sub 2:16:00 time qualify to be special guests.

AWARDS Awards to top ten finishers. Medals and official certificates to all finishers. Souvenirs to each participant.
COURSE RECORD Taisuke Kodama, Japan, 2:07:35 (1986).

TEMPERATURE 60°F (15°C)
CROWD 400,000
TERRAIN Completely flat.
COMPETITORS 220 from seventeen nations.
REFRESHMENTS AND SERVICES Water, sports drink every 5 kilometers; post-race blankets, sports drink.

ENTERTAINMENT Soccer game and merchandise lottery for audience in Workers' Stadium.
ADDITIONAL EVENTS Friday evening opening ceremony and welcoming party, awards ceremony.
UNUSUAL FEATURES A run around the heart of China; a live-TV audience of 220 million.

Chang'an Avenue. Buses and bicycles are stopped at intersections by policemen who will be rewarded with food allowances. Other than the souvenir pennants, all this audience can expect is a few minutes of entertainment and the chance to be part of a live television show watched by two hundred million of their countrymen and another twenty million TV viewers in Japan.

Children are lifted onto shoulders as the van passes through the square. When the broadcast truck goes past, banners flutter and free hands wave at the Japanese camera crew. Heads are turned by one of the leaders, a pale, reedy Englishman with red hair. The crowd respectfully observes the next twenty runners from sixteen nations—all sub-2:16:00 marathoners invited by the People's Republic of China. But when the first of two hundred Chinese runners arrive in Tienanmen Square, the spectators throw the pennants into overdrive and their reserve to the wind. Cheers roll up the avenue. A chant catches on and plays until the last runner is out of the sight of

Before 60,000 in Workers' Stadium, Shigeru Soh (number 12) strained to the 1985 finish ahead of Takeshi Soh, his twin—a proud TV picture for twenty million viewers in Japan.

Mao, who surely would have cringed at this joint venture between old enemies.

The Beijing International Marathon began in 1981. All agree to that, but which country came up with the idea is a sensitive topic. "It is something like a chicken and an egg," says Zuo Zhiyong of the China Sports Service Company. "Everyone thinks about it. The Japanese made the official proposal to us first."

Suntory Limited, a producer of whiskey, beer, wine, and juice products, hoped to tap the billion throats in China. The usual Suntory promotions—an award for mystery fiction, a classical music foundation, professional golf and tennis tournaments—would not fly in the Land of The Long March, Great Wall Country. A marathon seemed appropriate. Sponsorship began to pay off by race number three, when the company was allowed to open a Beijing office. The fourth race marked the establishment of a brewery in the city of Lian Yun Gang, and race five popped the cork of another in Beijing.

"Drinks served to the runners . . . will all be Suntory products," gushes the official race program. Other material rewards for the athletes remain secret. The near-capacity crowd of 60,000 in Workers' Stadium receives public rewards, however: Between the marathon's start and finish, the audience is entertained by a soccer game (Beijing versus Shanghai), the Beijing Marathon song ("Marathon is a contest of will and power; on the road of youth everyone strives for glory"), and by an audience lottery for which the grand prize is a Sanyo color-TV and VCR. Other giveaway items include ten radios, three hundred watches and thirty-six hundred T-shirts.

Alan Storey, coach of the British marathon team as well as advisor to the China Athletic Association, is concerned with who will win the race, which he follows on television in a VIP box. Hugh Jones, one of Storey's 1984 Olympians, leads most of the return trip from the China Theatre to the stadium via the south side of Tienanmen Square, site of Mao's mausoleum and the Chi'en Men Gate. With only two kilometers to go, Jones is passed by Japan's twin Soh brothers on the flower-lined Dongdaqiao Road.

"Due to economic and social pressures, it hasn't been socially acceptable in China to spend time training," Storey says as he awaits the ending. "That's changing. Eventually, instead of a couple of hundred Chinese who can run under three hours, there will be thousands."

"A mass marathon is a goal that everyone is working for," adds Kong Qingwen, a CSSC vice-chairman. Everyday in Beijing, the first steps are being taken at dawn.

Left, top: During the opening ceremony in the Great Hall of the People, the marathon team of the host nation parades onstage.

Left, bottom: Two days later, China's best race across Tienanmen Square before the Gate of Heavenly Peace, Chairman Mao, and a suddenly noisy crowd.

BERLIN, WEST GERMANY

BERLIN MARATHON

Of all the marathons not blessed with grand budgets and superstar names, the one most likely to survive far into the future is Berlin. The race attracts a field of 11,000, including four thousand foreigners from fifty-eight countries. Annually the numbers are on the rise (more Danes enter Berlin than any marathon in Denmark), and organizers expect 13,000 participants for their next edition. Among the superficial explanations for its appeal are the flat course, ideal fall weather, superb organization, and the large and vocal audience.

But a deeper reason exists, one having to do with symbols. There is no more fitting or inspiring locale for a long run than a city that in a generation's time was bombed, conquered, divided, and separated even from itself. West Berliners have sardonically come to call their part of the city "an island in the Red Sea." To the rest of the Free World, West Berlin represents mankind's indomitable spirit, which is also what marathons are about. Another inescapable connection is the Wall, which arrives literally and inevitably in Berlin. The course passes Checkpoint Charlie, the Allies' entry into East Berlin, just before the 16-kilometer point.

No one understood the symbolic lure of the Berlin Wall better than Race Director Horst Milde, a confectioner who considers its

James M. Ashworth of Great Britain in 1985 was the fastest ever to arrive at the burnt-out tower of the Kaiser-Wilhelm-Memorial Church, a symbol of the city's devastation in World War II.

Overleaf: When former Olympic champion Emil Zatopek fired the starter's gun in 1985, 11,000 sprang from the Reichstag, once site of the Weimar Republic's Houses of Parliament.

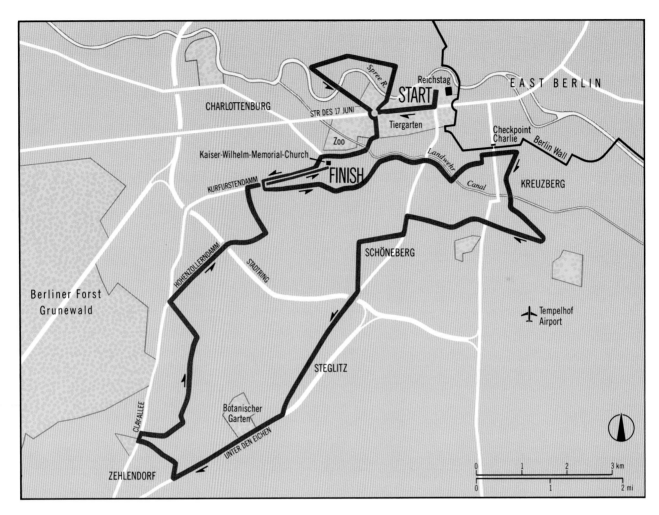

Berlin Marathon

ORGANIZER *Sport-Club Charlottenburg e.V.*
Meinekestrasse 13
D-1000 Berlin 15
West Germany
RACE DIRECTOR Horst Milde
DATE Last Sunday in September.
START 9:00 AM at the Reichstag, Platz der Republik.
FINISH Kaiser-Wilhelm-Memorial Church.
TIME LIMIT Five hours.
ELIGIBILITY Open to runners of all abilities; men must be eighteen years old by raceday, women must be twenty.

AWARDS Awards to top finishers in all age groups. Medals to all finishers. Results postcard, official certificate, and results magazine mailed to each finisher.
COURSE RECORDS Boguslaw Psujek, Poland, 2:11:03 (1986); Charlotte Teske, West Germany, 2:32:10 (1986).

TEMPERATURE 60°F (15°C)
CROWD 400,000
TERRAIN Completely flat.
COMPETITORS 11,000 from fifty-eight nations.

REFRESHMENTS AND SERVICES Water, tea, sports drink, bananas, oranges, and sponges every 5 kilometers; post-race blankets, massages, and showers.

ENTERTAINMENT A celebrity starter (often Olympic Champion Emil Zatopek) and ten bands along the way.
ADDITIONAL EVENTS Runners' mercantile expo and clinics, 6-kilometer Saturday morning Breakfast Jog for out-of-towners from Charlottenburg Palace to the 1936 Olympic Stadium, Saturday evening pasta party featuring live music, Saturday night prayer service at the Kaiser-Wilhelm-Memorial Church, awards ceremony and party.

inclusion "the first great victory" of the marathon. "When the Sport Club of Charlottenburg sought permission to take the race through the streets of the city in 1981, the idea was to show the runners the good and bad sides of Berlin," Milde says. "For Berliners, the Wall is the worst thing. But I knew that good public relations could be done with it. In America, you say marathoners run against the wall. We would offer a political description: Run against the Wall in Berlin."

Big-city marathons were popping up all over Europe, and in 1981 a rival race was launched close to Milde's home in West Berlin, and in Frankfurt. But Milde had a unique hook, he hoped. All he had to do was convince the American, British, and French governments and the local police department to go along. "Checkpoint Charlie was forbidden," says Milde. "Runners would never be allowed near it, I was told. But I had a friend who knew the political man at the American Embassy. A private supper was arranged. I explained my problem to the deputy ambassador. 'We have to find a solution,' he agreed. In ten days he worked everything out."

The police believed that cars came first and they didn't want to close the streets. Milde flew the police commissioner to the Stockholm Marathon before accepting a no. "He saw that the policemen there loved the race, and all wanted to work that day. Afterward, he shook my hand and said, 'Congratulations. You won. We'll do it.'"

Nobody does it better than Berlin. Attention to detail is astonishing, even by German standards. A police boat even patrols the River Spree for discarded water bottles. A movie theater shows *The Loneliness of the Long Distance Runner* and *Marathon Man* all raceweek. The finish area on Kurfürstendamm is equipped with hot showers. Among the sales items at the runners' expo are teddy bears wearing miniature Berlin Marathon T-shirts. On the eve of the event there is a runners-only prayer service at the Kaiser-Wilhelm-Memorial Church. Each entrant receives a Berlin guidebook captioned in four languages. Computer-results cards containing kilometers-per-hour and average-per-kilometer times are mailed to each finisher raceday afternoon. The two million residents of West Berlin are kept informed of the Twelve Golden Rules for Spectators, a list that includes (rule 1) having to applaud, (rule 7) removing parked cars from the course, and (rule 11) offering toilets to runners in need.

The 400,000 spectators who line the loop from the Reichstag Building to Kurfürstendamm are equally familiar with the lyrics of "Marathonlied," written by humorist Ingo Insterburg. "Marathoners are running through the streets of the city; the smokers and drinkers are looking with great big eyes."

There is even a well-worn marathon joke: Why doesn't the Berlin Marathon go through East Berlin? Because 10,000 would start and 20,000 would finish.

The success of the event has played a joke on Milde. It has made him famous. "A team of thirty men put on this race, but the media only wants to talk about one," he says forlornly. "It is against my nature to be in public."

One night, Milde was awakened by a phone call. A stranger announced that he had just become engaged to a woman he had met in the race, and asked Milde if he would witness the marriage. "I agreed, even though it meant putting on a tie. We have to do anything we can for the marathon."

Left: Only nine kilometers into the race and in no need of a break, marathoners pass the Kranzler, Berlin's renowned coffee house on Kurfürstendamm.

Each tulip in his cap representing a Berlin Marathon successfully finished, Frans Rutten, a runner from Holland, predicts a fifth while his starting-line companion demonstrates less self-confidence.

BERMUDA

BERMUDA INTERNATIONAL MARATHON

Thousands of sailors and scores of prop-plane pilots have disappeared in the Bermuda Triangle, an enigmatic swatch of Sargasso Seascape between Miami, Puerto Rico, and Bermuda. Among the vanished are the crews of five US Navy bombers and the search party that was sent after them one baffling day in 1945. The final transmission from the squadron leader was eerie: "Everything is wrong. Even the ocean doesn't look as it should."

Commercial travel to Bermuda has been quite safe; no jetliner or cruise ship has been lost. But much about the destination remains illogical. Only six hundred miles from the continental US, Bermuda is a self-governing colony of the British Commonwealth. Except for its narrow, walled lanes, there is nothing very British about the twenty-one-mile strip of land. The vegetation is semi-tropical; the buildings are painted in warm pastels; unlike residents of the Mother Country, the 60,000 Bermudians hope for rain, their only water source; the climate is pleasant year-round, with the seasons more marked by tourist flow than temperature change.

January is an off month when many hotels close for renovations, and unemployment figures and island fever climb to yearly highs. International fun-and-games help pass the time. There are bridge,

chess, golf, sailing, and square-dance competitions, as well as a weekend given over to a 10-kilometer footrace and a marathon. The shorter event, on Saturday, is an annual hit that usually includes Norway's Grete Waitz among its nearly one thousand entrants.

Sunday is something else. From afar, the Bermuda International Marathon appears to be a delightful run past all sorts of charming, sophisticated diversions: horse-drawn carriages touring Queen's Park, windsurfers gliding over the aquamarine waters beyond North Shore Road, golfers ambling the fairways of Tucker's Town, and swimmers riding the waves of John Smith's Bay. But that is an illusion as off-course as the doomed Navy bombers.

The terrain comes as a shock to many of the 150 starters. The Bermuda Track & Field Association promotes the event as "the best kept secret in road running," a line appropriately enigmatic. The

A tranquil seascape on North Shore Road near Devonshire Dock at 7 kilometers belies the difficulty of the course, where spectators are as likely as runners to encounter a wall.

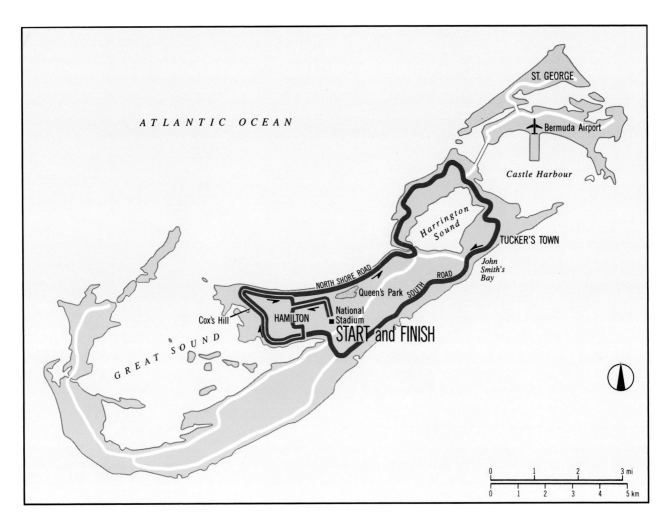

Bermuda International Marathon

ORGANIZER *Bermuda Track and Field
Association
Post Office Box 397
Devonshire 4
Bermuda*
RACE DIRECTOR Clive Longe
DATE Third Sunday in January.
START 10:00 AM at Frog Lane, National
Stadium.
FINISH National Stadium.
TIME LIMIT None.
ELIGIBILITY Open to runners of all abil-
ities; runners must be sixteen years old
by raceday.

AWARDS Awards to top finishers in all age
groups; also awards to top teams and
local runners. Trophies to first two hundred finishers. Official certificate to each
finisher.

COURSE RECORDS Andy Holden, Great
Britain, 2:15:20 (1980); Kiki Sweigart,
USA, 2:43:09 (1981).

TEMPERATURE 65°F (18°C)
CROWD 15,000
TERRAIN Fifty-two hills, the most difficult
being Cox's Hill (a ¼-mile climb at 4
miles and 23 miles).
COMPETITORS 150 from five nations.
REFRESHMENTS AND SERVICES Water drink
every 3 miles; post-race blankets, electrolyte drink, juice.

ENTERTAINMENT Bagpiper on Cox's Hill.
ADDITIONAL EVENTS Saturday morning 10-
kilometer race, awards ceremony, disco
party.
UNUSUAL FEATURE The most hills of any
major, international marathon.

marathon brochure does not disclose the difficulty of the journey. One of those caught unaware was Jean-Marc DesRochers, a fifty-eight-year-old government translator from Ottawa, who initially discovered the Bermuda Marathon in the index of a book titled *How To Run Your First Marathon.* By the time DesRochers touched down in Bermuda, he had managed three marathons and considered himself conditioned to enjoy an escape route from the Canadian winter.

"I assumed that a race around an island would be flat," DesRochers said. "What seemed like a wonderful idea when I was up to here in snow became not so good when I went over the course by bus. I realized I would have to walk many of the hills that go up." He abandoned all hope of breaking four hours and, satisfied with finishing, covered the distance in 4:43:08. "After this," he said of the experience, "everything will seem easy."

The layout contains an incredible fifty-two hills—that's two per mile, not just a full, but a stacked, deck. The trick is not to think about them, even if you happen to be a highly trained athlete. "I started out wanting to count each one," says American Sally Zimmer of Team Adidas. "But it didn't take long to drop the idea. Why get depressed?"

It's impossible to blank out Cox's Hill, a steep quarter-mile that is merely a nuisance at four miles but a killer when it comes around again at twenty-three. A bagpiper does his best for the runners on both trips, and unofficial volunteers offer juice, beer, and even Bloody Marys at the top. "All those people kept me from giving up," says DesRochers.

Nothing is easy about the Bermuda Marathon, not even coming in last. Robert D. Clark, a fifty-two-year-old attorney from New York City, had traveled seventeen miles when suddenly he was confronted by strangers. "A taxi pulled up," Clark recalled. "The three passengers looked at me with concern. 'You think you're all right? You still have a long way to go,' one said. Not words I needed to hear. The very strong implication was that the sensible thing for me to do was drop out and accept a ride."

The scene was repeated twice more along South Road, but Clark stubbornly continued his long struggle to the National Stadium, where he was greeted by the strangers. "You screwed us up. What a pain you were," he was told. He had unwittingly spoiled a group prank to place two guys running as Millard P. Billingsgate, age unknown, from the USA, at the bottom of the list of finishers; the pranksters had been unable to remove Clark from the running. Despite mysterious requests to the contrary, Clark was one disoriented visitor to the Triangle who had refused to disappear.

The 1986 leaders, including Bermuda's best, Ray Swan (number 7), climb Frog Lane—one hill down, fifty-one to go.

BOSTON, MASSACHUSETTS

BOSTON MARATHON

S ome two hours after the winners of the ninetieth Boston Marathon have been determined, the audience in Copley Square waits for a slightly stooped, seventy-eight-year-old legend named John A. Kelley to once again both steal and close the show. There is comfort in this. Ted Williams is long retired and Arthur Fiedler is dead, but "Old John" is out there somewhere.

Still, signs of change hang in the damp air. The finish line has been moved to within the shadow of the John Hancock Tower, headquarters of the race's brand-new corporate sponsor. Hancock billboards hurrah the news that "Boston is Back." A high-rise video screen entertains a bleacher crowd with live race coverage. Instead of the gloomy underground garage of yesteryear, finishers repair to six yellow-and-white-striped tents. And most startling of all, a $250,000 purse is being pitched around.

Only a few raceday traditions can be counted on at Boston—the morning baseball game at Fenway Park, the noon Patriot's Day start, and Kelley, who has been running Boston longer than most runners have been alive. He won the race in 1935 and 1945, placed second in 1934, 1946, and five years in between, and dropped out in 1928, 1932, and 1956. If he makes it, this will be his fifty-second Boston

Above: England's Geoff Smith in 1985.

Right: Robert de Castella on Heartbreak Hill in 1986.

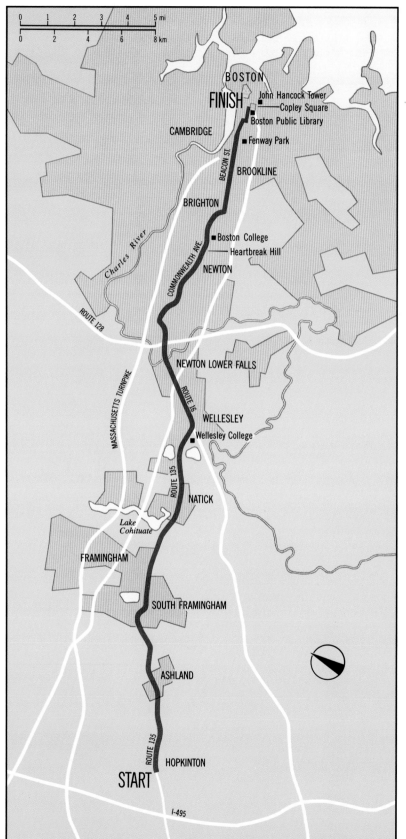

Boston Marathon

ORGANIZER *Boston Athletic Association*
17 Main Street
Hopkinton, MA 01748
USA
RACE DIRECTOR Guy Morse
DATE Third Monday in April (Patriot's Day).
START 12:00 noon at Hopkinton.
FINISH Copley Square, Boston.
TIME LIMIT Four hours.
ELIGIBILITY Since the previous Patriot's Day, runners must have finished a TAC-sanctioned marathon within the following times to qualify as entrants: 3:00:00 for men under 40, 3:10:00 for men 40–49, 3:20:00 for men 50–59, 3:30:00 for men 60 and over and women under 40, 3:40:00 for women 40–49, 3:50:00 for women 50–59, 4:00:00 for women 60 and over.

AWARDS Awards to top finishers in all age groups. Medals to all finishers. Results postcard, official certificate, and results magazine mailed to each finisher.
COURSE RECORDS Robert de Castella, Australia, 2:07:51 (1986); Joan Benoit, USA, 2:22:43 (1983).

TEMPERATURE 60°F (15°C)
CROWD 900,000
TERRAIN Mostly downhill for first 6 miles, the four Newton hills (16 miles to 21.5 miles), downhill toward the finish (21.5 miles to 25 miles).
COMPETITORS 4,850 from thirty-eight nations.
REFRESHMENTS AND SERVICES Water every 2 miles; post-race blankets, snacks, juice and soft drinks, massages.

ENTERTAINMENT Giant video screen at the finish.
ADDITIONAL EVENTS Runners' mercantile expo and clinics, Sunday evening pasta party, awards ceremony, disco party.
UNUSUAL FEATURES Qualification standards for the masses; the best crowd in marathoning; the oldest annual marathon.

finish. Kelley is more than the unofficial grand marshal of marathoning's oldest parade.

TV commentator Marty Liquori put things in perspective when he said, "No other marathon in the world could have a Johnny Kelley in it." (Boston has two, actually. John J. "Young John" Kelley—no relation—is the 1957 champion and a frequent participant.) But the elder Kelley embodies a long, glorious past.

Boston was *the* marathon for four-score years before completing a marathon became *the thing* to do. The starting fields flooded with trendies once the running boom struck. When 7,900 entrants appeared in 1979, the Boston Athletic Association instituted rigorous qualifying standards (see box). Boston became the goal for serious-minded amateurs; the professionals, though, soon ran elsewhere.

After three years of declining prestige—not to mention a string of embarrassments starting when Rosie Ruiz was crowned the 1980 champion after allegedly running only a mile—the BAA finally admitted in July 1985 that more than tradition was needed to lure elite athletes. The eleven-member Board of Governors announced that it would award prize money and signed John Hancock Financial Services to a ten-year, ten-million-dollar deal, guaranteeing top tal-

The calm before the boom: The 1975 Hopkinton start contained elbowroom between the 2,000 runners and a grammar school teacher named Bill Rodgers, who was just two hours and nine minutes from fame.

No marathon crowd is as spirited as Boston's, which for nearly a century has been high on the April event.

ent right up to the centennial race. Suddenly, the future looked, well, rosy.

For the 4,800 official qualifiers in 1986, the payoff remained considerable—an authorized tour of the Grande Dame herself. Among the notable landmarks strewn en route are: the forsythia bush in Hopkinton where Roberta Gibb Bingay, the first woman to run Boston, hid before the 1966 start (women were not officially recognized as runners by the BAA until 1972); the railroad crossing in South Framingham where a freight delayed most of the field of 1907; Natick's Lake Cochituate, where Ellison "Tarzan" Brown abandoned the lead for a swim in 1941; Newton Lower Falls, where a sprinting Labrador retriever veered into the leaders in 1961 and knocked "Young John" Kelley to the pavement; Boston College, where Bill Rodgers knelt to tie a shoelace, one of five full stops on the way to a 2:09:55 American record in 1975; Charlesgate Street near Fenway, where Ruiz is assumed to have hopped the marathon express.

And then there is famed Heartbreak Hill (20.6 to 21.4 miles), which rates a paragraph of its own. In 1936, "Old John" Kelley caught a faltering Brown on the last of the Newton climbs and tapped his rival on the shoulder. The gesture inspired Brown's charge to victory and the christening of Heartbreak by the *Boston Globe*'s Jerry Nason.

A half-century later, here comes Kelley again, alive and kicking to the finish. A roar rattles Copley Square. "We love you, Johnny," someone yells. Kelley is cold, wet, and feeling sick to his stomach, discomforts he keeps to himself. He grins and waves sore arms above his head during the final yards past the Boston Public Library.

"I'm thrilled," he tells his sister after a post-race hug. "I didn't walk at all." Tradition too is satisfied. Now that Kelley has gone by, everyone can go home.

Rodgers ran his first Boston in a ragtag T-shirt with the name of his track club hand-lettered across the front, but six years and four wins later he is resplendent in his own clothing line.

CHICAGO, ILLINOIS

AMERICA'S MARATHON/ CHICAGO

Among the eight thousand amateur runners assembled in Chicago's Daley Plaza one October Sunday in 1985 was Dave Dyer, a thirty-six-year-old sports columnist for the *Daily Journal* in Kankakee, Illinois. This was to be his twenty-second marathon—his goal is to complete fifty by age fifty—and he had supposed that by now very little could dazzle him. From the small-town charm of Hurley, Wisconsin, to the Communist capital city of Moscow, Dyer had run it all. He expected the immodestly named America's Marathon/Chicago to be a three-hour tour of a familiar city; another 26.2 miles conveniently notched. As he lined up for the dual start, edging ahead of his honor-system time slot ("like everyone else"), he scanned the mayor, the brass band, and the flags of nations. No big thing. But when he happened to glance at a nearby runner, Dyer crashed head-on into fantasy. Suddenly he was face to face with the Walter Mitty Factor.

"Five feet away was Ingrid Kristiansen, the world-record holder," Dyer recalls. "She was talking to someone. I was being a runner not a reporter, so I didn't ask her anything. Anyway, I was too awed. I began thinking that this was pretty neat. Here I was (his best time is 2:51:25) standing beside a world-class runner. There isn't any other

Above: Steve Jones. Right: Despite the sponsor's attempts at community involvement, Chicago just goes about its business.

MARATHONS

event in sports that would give someone like me the chance to compete with the very best. Feeling exhilarated, I spent the final moments before the gun looking for Joan Benoit."

Big names and big bucks distinguish America's Marathon/Chicago. Beginning in 1984, runners with reputations as soaring as the Sears Tower have gathered in Chicago for racing's richest payoff. The dream sponsor, Beatrice Companies, Inc., changed the economics of marathoning by pouring five million dollars into the event in two successive years (1985 and 1986), much of it to fund star wars with New York.

"Until we came along, New York was a great environment that didn't have to pay anyone very much," says Bob Bright, the race's executive director. "We do open appearance payments and a recruitment lobbying effort. Fred Lebow keeps promoting the New York image as worth money. I don't think the athletes agree." Said Joan Benoit Samuelson after her 1985 Chicago victory: "Beatrice has turned America's Marathon into the world's marathon. This is where the competition is."

Samuelson was Bright's biggest triumph that year, a celebrity who outshone and outearned even the likes of Norway's Kristiansen (paid $25,000 to appear, $25,000 for placing second) and Great Britain's Steve Jones (paid $30,000 to appear, $35,000 for winning, and

On the way to the second fastest marathon ever run, Jones's 1985 solo performance inspired a dash of audience participation.

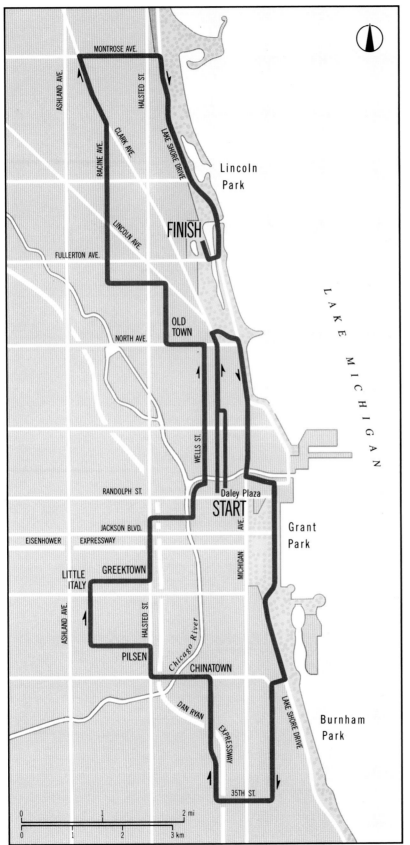

ORGANIZER *America's Marathon/Chicago*
214 West Erie Street
Chicago, IL 60610
USA

EXECUTIVE DIRECTOR Bob Bright

DATE Third or fourth Sunday in October.

START 8:45 AM at Daley Plaza.

FINISH Lincoln Park.

TIME LIMIT Five-and-a-half hours.

ELIGIBILITY Open to runners of all abilities; runners must be eighteen years old by raceday.

AWARDS Awards to top finishers in all age groups, also awards to top corporate teams. Medals to all finishers; roses to women finishers. Results postcard, official certificate, and results magazine mailed to each finisher.

COURSE RECORDS Steve Jones, Great Britain, 2:07:13 (1985); Joan Benoit, USA, 2:21:21 (1985).

TEMPERATURE 55°F (13°C)

CROWD 150,000

TERRAIN Completely flat.

COMPETITORS 8,000 from sixty nations.

REFRESHMENTS AND SERVICES Water and electrolyte drink every 2 miles; post-race blankets, snacks, mineral water, orange juice, soft drinks, massages.

ENTERTAINMENT Twenty bands, belly dancer, cheerleaders, choirs, Dragon Dancers, martial-arts display, organ grinder, tumblers.

ADDITIONAL EVENTS Runners' mercantile expo, clinics, Saturday evening pasta party, awards ceremony, post-race party.

UNUSUAL FEATURE Recently the best annual field in marathoning.

$10,000 for setting a course record). For the Olympic marathon gold medalist, Bright set up an eighteen-month, $130,000 contract with Dole (the pineapple people). Her win and course record were worth $45,000.

Bright enjoys his annual battles with Lebow. "The rivalry is good for the sport," he says. "We have fun with it. There's just one rule: We don't poach each other's champions."

Combat comes naturally to Bright. He survived thirty months as a Marine advisor to a Vietnamese reconnaissance unit. In peacetime, he has trained and raced huskies for nearly twenty years, placing as high as twenty-second driving his team in the 1,200-mile Alaskan Iditarod Trail Sled Dog Race.

"I have dogs with great hearts and heads but who don't have the equipment to go fast. Others have great ability but no head. You have to reach inside and find what's going on in there. The motivating factor. It's the same with runners. Take Benoit. You look at this meek thing. But if you reach over and peel back Joan's skin, there's the 'Alien'. She's one tough little lady. She has this mystique where the other athletes are afraid of her. I knew it would take more than money to get her. I had to appeal to her competitiveness. I ignored her completely until I had the best women's field since Los Angeles. There was no way she could turn that down. I had painted her into a corner."

The same may be said of America's Marathon/Chicago, a race cornered in a city—"a meat and potatoes town," Bright calls it— that doesn't much care. A crowd of only 150,000 shows up, a far cry from the magic made by a million New Yorkers. Community involvement is not enhanced by the fact that Bright resides on a farm in upstate New York, and the two thousand "volunteers" who work the event are Beatrice employees. Money can't buy love.

Certainly the conglomerate has tried. In 1985, Beatrice spent $200,000 to improve attendance. It published 250,000 spectator guides, gave away thousands of spectator T-shirts, commissioned a mural, recruited neighborhood captains, and placed a Greek belly dancer, Chinese lion-and-dragon dancers, Scottish bagpipers, and a Jamaican reggae band along the route. It even handed out do-it-yourself noisemakers—kazoos, maracas, tambourines, and whistles. But that season Chicago was dancing only to "The Super Bowl Shuffle."

"The ethnic neighborhoods were kind of neat, but the highlight for me was waiting for the start," says Dyer, who would always remember his marathon number twenty-two as his close encounter with a marathon star.

Superstars signed on in 1985—World Champion Robert de Castella (who finished third behind Jones and Djiboutian Robleh Djama in 2:08:48) and Olympic Champion Joan Benoit Samuelson (who beat Ingrid Kristiansen of Norway and Portugal's Rosa Mota in the American-record time of 2:21:21).

DUBLIN, IRELAND

DUBLIN CITY MARATHON

Done in by the hills of North Dublin, the runner stopped in the city's Fairview District, three miles from the finish. He ignored audience requests to carry on, skulked off the road, and lumbered, head-down, along a sidewalk. After a block or so—far enough for his numb mind to begin to ponder the long odds of finding a taxi—an elderly woman took his arm and asked if he was in need of a drink. He nodded and watched her hurry into a brick house. Out she came holding a glass with both hands. Expecting water, he gulped the contents: Whiskey! he tasted too late. Too tired to be alarmed, he stood still and waited for the reaction, which would no doubt stagger him backward and drop him to the pavement as though he had taken a shot in the gut, which was true, in a sense. But all he felt was a spreading warmth. Somewhere inside might also be the stirrings of a third or fourth wind, he supposed. He thanked the woman and rejoined the race, answering her applause with a wave.

This is a story that Race Administrator Ned Sweeney enjoys telling about his Dublin City Marathon. "In Ireland water is only to keep you alive, but a drink is a *drink*." He continues, "Could have killed the man, but it's the thought that counts. Came out all right in

Optimistic beyond reason, the well intentioned message on the left is not news to cheer marathoners, Gerard included.

the end. He finished."

Dubliners always get their marathoners through, one way or another: Through October weather that is often foul; through a course that until recently contained five steep hills and still climbs 380 grueling feet; through scenery that consists mostly of subsidy housing, working-class neighborhoods, and a blustery sea front. Each year 200,000 spectators assemble along a jagged loop from Merrion Square to Stephen's Green. It is a family group—babies in prams, kids with signs, adults holding dogs—which entirely justifies the race's corny moniker, "The Friendly Marathon." No crowd has more effectively lifted spirits and footsteps. Ninety-six percent of Dublin's starters have made it home, the highest completion rate of all the world's mass marathons.

"There's a bit of the extrovert in us," says Sweeney, a ship broker

"I've dreamed of having the audience to myself," said Dubliner Dick Hooper, and by the time he reached the 23-mile point in Ballybough in 1985 he had a four minute lead and a wish come true.

for Shell Oil who has been described as a talkative little leprechaun of a man. "We like to welcome people. The warmth of Dubliners is what makes this marathon special. The runners are encouraged all the way round. They *have* to finish."

The encouragement is nicely put, as would be expected in James Joyce's hometown. No one yells "Come on, you can do it!" because only God can be sure of that. Dubliners choose to shout "Fair play to you!" and "You're doing as well as you can!" Carried along by such sensible comments was one Guy Cummane, a dental surgeon from the Isle of Man. "I've just turned forty, so I suppose I had plenty of motivation to do the run in any case," he said after the 1985 race. "But the Irish were very good-natured and demonstrated a great deal of good will. I was inspired by their honest appreciation of my efforts."

To ensure an appealing crowd, Sweeney and his fellow clubbers from the Business Houses' Athletic Association avoided the posh sections of Dublin when they first organized the event in 1980. "We were all runners," says Sweeney. "We knew the stockbroker types wouldn't cheer on sweaty bodies or stand at the side of the road giving out water. The affluent are not the serving kind. We took the race to people who made up in humor and enthusiasm what they lacked in finances."

What Sweeney and the boys from the BHAA were ignorant about was the Big Picture—the mesmerizing effect the Dublin City Marathon would have on their countrymen. That first year they printed five hundred entry forms; they received two thousand entry requests. Three years later, 11,500 runners entered the race, then the third largest marathon field anywhere. "We trailed only London and New York," Sweeney says. "New York's Fred Lebow called our numbers 'mindboggling'. He was right. Only three million people lived in the Republic. The only explanation was one of our national characteristics: We do everything in excess."

The size of the field has stabilized since those giddy Marathon Mondays, as the bank-holiday racedate came to be called throughout Ireland, when every hamlet had somebody running and there was barely elbowroom in the curves. Now seven thousand marathoners fill the streets, and there is plenty of space for another vivid story. "After this year's race a British coach came up to me," chirrups the leprechaun. " 'I have one small complaint,' he said. 'A young chap ran onto the course and tried to pull the knickers off one of my girls. She was in sixth place at the time.' I told him I'd investigate, but how can I be responsible for every ruffian in Dublin?"

The comparatively small crowd of 200,000 holds the record for effective encouragement—ninety-six percent of the field finishes.

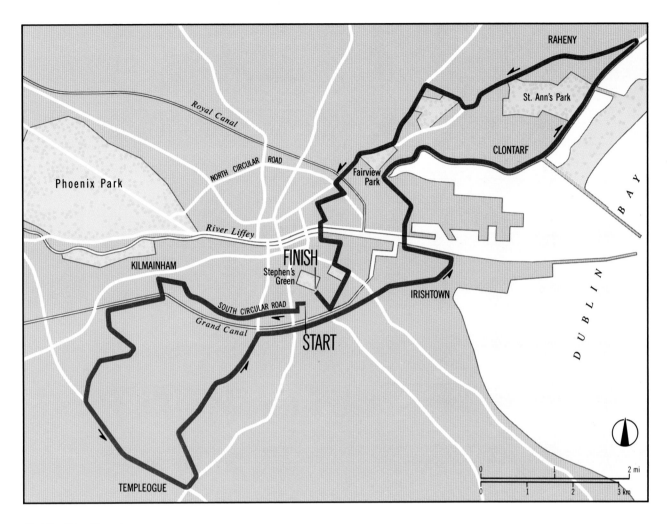

Dublin City Marathon

ORGANIZER *Business Houses' Athletic*
    Association
    3 Fitzwilliam Place
    Dublin 2
    Ireland
RACE DIRECTOR Ned Sweeney
DATE Last Monday in October.
START 11:00 AM at Merrion Square.
FINISH Stephen's Green.
TIME LIMIT Six hours.
ELIGIBILITY Open to runners of all abilities.

AWARDS Awards to top finishers in all age groups. Plaques to all finishers.
COURSE RECORDS Jerry Kiernan, Ireland,

2:13:45 (1982); Debbie Mueller, USA, 2:40:57 (1982).

TEMPERATURE 50°F (10°C)
CROWD 200,000
TERRAIN Flat for the first 4 miles and the last 3. In between is a gradual climb to 6 miles, a ½-mile rise on Howth Road (18.5 to 19 miles), and a short rise at Canal Bridge (23.5 miles).
COMPETITORS 7,000 from thirty nations.
REFRESHMENTS AND SERVICES Water every 2 miles; post-race blankets, snack, mineral water, coffee, tea, massages.

ENTERTAINMENT Three bands along the way.
ADDITIONAL EVENT Awards ceremony and party featuring Irish traditional music.
UNUSUAL FEATURES The highest completion rate (ninety-six percent) in mass marathoning, best-costume competition.

Although only three million people live in the Republic, the giddy Dublin Marathon has drawn as many as 11,500 to the start on Marathon Monday.

FUKUOKA, JAPAN

FUKUOKA INTERNATIONAL OPEN MARATHON CHAMPIONSHIP

The eighth-largest city in Japan—Fukuoka—is two hours southwest of Tokyo as the JAL commuter jets fly. Businessmen make the trip, not tourists. Regional sales is what Fukuoka is all about, being the commercial hub of Kyushu Island. Companies do not originate in town, but their branch offices prosper there. Even Fukuoka's famous marathon did not open in the city. For a decade or so it toured Japan before Tokyo headquarters, the sponsoring Asahi Shimbun Publishing Company, shipped it to their office in Fukuoka, there to evolve into an international success.

One Sunday each December, thirty-five million TV viewers tune in to watch as many as 150 male runners—all of whom have earned the exposure by meeting a 2:27:00 qualifying standard—crisscross downtown Fukuoka. The show has created one national legend, four-time winner Toshihiko Seko, and beamed word to Japanese households of the names Frank Shorter, a quadruple winner himself, Bill Rodgers, and Robert de Castella. Still Japan's premier 42.195-kilometer race, the Fukuoka International Open Marathon Championship was the most prestigious annual roadrace in the world for nearly two decades, the one only the very best could hope to win. The event was notable solely for the athletes assembled by the Japan

Amateur Athletic Federation. No one ever claimed that the locale added to the appeal, except to say that the roads were flat and the weather cool. On its biggest day of the year, the city of Fukuoka seemed incidental.

One of the city's million residents, Tadayuki Ikeno, an Asahi Shimbun executive, looks bewildered when asked to describe highlights along the course. "This is an urban race," he says. "We have a large audience—maybe 400,000—instead of beautiful scenery." It is enough to add that the five-kilometer checkpoints are found at spots like the Hirayama Barbershop, Plaza Parking Lot, Shirohama Housing Complex, and Nafuko Supermarket. No matter. Only fun-runners require an aesthetic shot in the leg every now and again to keep them going, and they do not exist in this race.

What does matter is that overseas marathon stars suddenly stopped accepting JAAF invitations to compete in Fukuoka. The crisis hit in 1984, when media events in Chicago and New York declared a bidding war on one another and fired off escalating

Although prestige has declined, attention to detail remains a Fukuoka hallmark, as evidenced by the uniformed officials assembled at the awards ceremony.

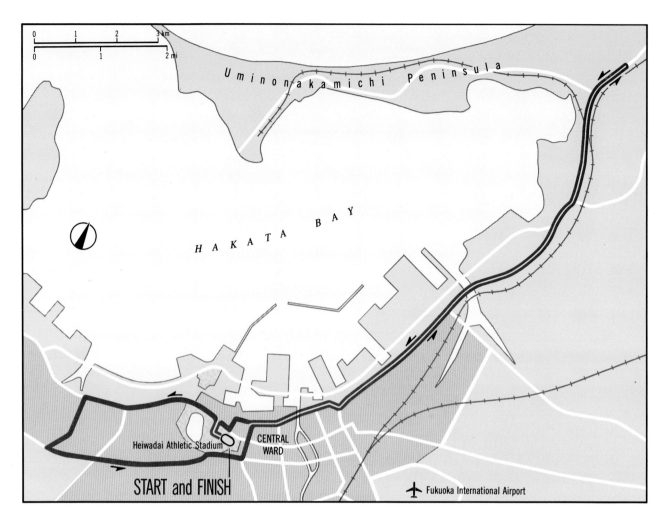

Fukuoka International Open Marathon Championship

ORGANIZER *Japan Amateur Athletic
Federation
1-1-1 Jinnan
Shibuya-ku
Tokyo 150
Japan*
RACE DIRECTOR Hiroaki Chosa
DATE First Sunday in December.
START 12:15 PM in Heiwadai Athletic
Stadium.
FINISH Heiwadai Athletic Stadium.
TIME LIMIT Located at 5-kilometer inter-
vals, checking stations close fifteen min-
utes after the passing of the first runner
on the outward course and thirty minutes
after the passing of the first runner on
the return course.
ELIGIBILITY Open to male runners who
have achieved at least a 2:27:00 mar-
athon time; foreign runners with a sub
2:13:00 time qualify to be guests of the
Japanese Amateur Athletic Federation.

AWARDS Awards to top ten finishers. Official certificate to each finisher.
COURSE RECORD Robert de Castella, Australia, 2:08:18 (1981).

TEMPERATURE 55°F (13°C)
CROWD 400,000
TERRAIN Flat except for short grade by
Heiwadai Athletic Stadium.
COMPETITORS 150 from nine nations.
REFRESHMENTS AND SERVICES Water and
sports drink every 5 kilometers beginning
at 16-kilometer mark, sponges midway
between each water station; post-race
blankets, sports drink, massages, showers.

ENTERTAINMENT Military band at the start
and finish; fireworks signal that the race
has started, the first runner has reached
the turnabout, and the first runner has
finished.
ADDITIONAL EVENTS Saturday afternoon
opening ceremony, awards ceremony.
UNUSUAL FEATURES The most difficult
qualifying standard in marathoning

appearance and prize monies as well as bonus incentives. Something drastic had to be done. Race officials settled on a course change, the first major alteration in twenty years. They scratched the only pretty stretch of the run, 10 kilometers of stereo seascape along the Uminonakamichi Peninsula. "Too much wind," explains Ikeno. "They are hoping for a fast time to get the top people back."

Hardly the answer these money-minded days. The traditional Fukuoka Marathon handout is not likely to impress hard-bitten bottom-liners either; every invited runner receives a fifty-page souvenir scrapbook. "So what can my client expect?" agents are fond of asking. "Newspaper clippings? In Japanese?" The JAAF takes its second initial seriously, allowing itself donations only to sister federations that send teams to Fukuoka—a Nissan minibus for Ethiopia is one recent example. "Amateur" still retains its definition in Japan, where tradition is dear and change comes slowly. For the moment, the JAAF does not sanction prize money for individuals. The agents put Fukuoka on hold.

Once upon a time, the Fukuoka Marathon was regarded as generous. It was the first marathon to offer deserving foreigners a free ride. A 2:12:00 time guaranteed a travel package brimming with first-class competition, tickets, hotels, and service. "The organizers made you feel very special, as though you were the only one in the race," says Australia's Derek Clayton, the former world-record holder who won Fukuoka in 1967. "Everything was taken care of. There were no hassles or worries. You could spend all week in a daze, left to think about what was important—the run. Nothing has changed. The caring for detail is still astonishing."

On raceday afternoon, a crowd jammed Heiwadai Athletic Stadium's squat grandstand, spread along a grass embankment, and waited for the winner. Uniformed schoolgirls were out on the running track practicing their floral march to the victory platform. Men dressed in identical windbreakers and hats arranged medals and trophies just-so on a linen tablecloth. At last all eyes turned to Masanari Shintaku. Three thousand spectators welcomed their countryman with a shrill cheer, waving small, patriotic flags with a fury. Shintaku grimaced all the way around the track, straining to maintain his ten-second lead over Hiromi Taniguchi. Shintaku crossed the tape with fists in the air, fireworks in the sky, and 2:09:51 on the clock.

Fukuoka always produces an impressive sales figure. But some major marketing decisions will have to be made back in Tokyo before the current world-record holder commutes to the city on marathon business.

The Japanese Amateur Athletic Federation takes its name literally, banning prize money and leaving recent winners like Masanari Shintaku in a position of prominence only among elite amateurs.

Overleaf: Three thousand spectators jammed tiny Heiwadai Athletic Stadium in 1985 to cheer the start of the twentieth running.

HELSINKI, FINLAND

HELSINKI CITY MARATHON

Only blocks apart in the capital city of Helsinki are memorials to Finland's two most famous men. The bust of composer Jean Sibelius, jaw set and brow furrowed, faces a stand of birches as though imagining the towering sounds of his seven symphonies. Before Olympic Stadium, a smaller-than-life statue of Paavo Nurmi runs full-stride displaying the style that won nine gold medals at three Olympic Games.

"To the rest of the world, Finland is known for Sibelius, sauna, and Nurmi," says Raija Ylonen, secretary of the Finnish Amateur Athletic Association, whose offices are located midway between Sibelius Park and Nurmi Avenue. "Sibelius, sauna, Nurmi," she repeats. "It has become a joke with us."

Finns mock the simplistic perceptions of outsiders as a matter of self-defense. Ever since the twelfth century, when Sweden's King Erik IX began the habit of using Finland as a battleground, the country has been trashed by its neighbors. In recent peacetime, the abuse is verbal rather than territorial. Finnish jokes make the rounds in Scandinavia.

Slow of speech and reticent by nature, Finns are easy to tease. Sometimes they openly ask for it. When Finland proudly announced

At about 25 kilometers runners glimpse Senate Square and the Cathedral of Helsinki, a multi-domed building symbolizing the city since 1852.

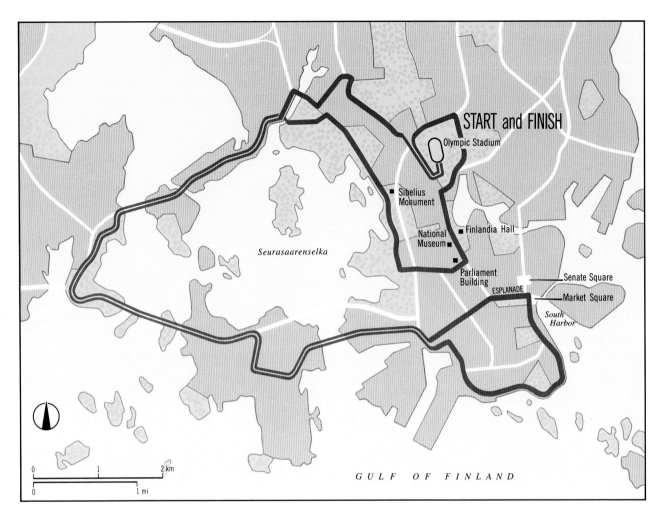

Helsinki City Marathon

ORGANIZER *Finnish Amateur Athletic*
Association
Radiokatu 12
00240 Helsinki
Finland
RACE DIRECTOR Pertti Raunio
DATE First Saturday in August.
START 5:00 PM at Olympic Stadium.
FINISH Olympic Stadium.
TIME LIMIT Five-and-a-half hours.
ELIGIBILITY Open to runners of all abil-
ities; runners must be eighteen years old
by raceday.

AWARDS Awards to top finishers in all age
groups, also awards to top local teams.
Medals to all finishers. Results magazine
mailed to each finisher.
COURSE RECORDS Jorma Sippola, Finland,
2:15:36 (1985); Sinikka Kesikitalo,
Finland, 2:39:43 (1983).

TEMPERATURE 65°F (18°C)
CROWD 100,000
TERRAIN Gentle hills, most noticeably a
gradual 3-kilometer rise (12 K to 15 K)
and a 1-kilometer climb beginning at 37 K.
COMPETITORS 4,000 from twenty-five nations.
REFRESHMENTS AND SERVICES Water and
sports drink at least every 5 kilometers;
post-race oranges and pickles, sports
drink, juice.

ENTERTAINMENT Jazz band at the start
and halfway, rock band at the finish.
ADDITIONAL EVENTS Runners' mercantile
expo, Friday evening pancake-and-straw-
berry-jam party for foreign runners,
awards ceremony.
UNUSUAL FEATURE A capital-city race
featuring nature-made scenery.

a recent high-tech contract to build a toilet-paper factory for the Russians, reams of laughter rolled in from the West. As for high times, thousands celebrate the coming of June in Helsinki by watching an honored newlywed couple set fire to an enormous pile of old boats.

An example of functional, graceful Finnish design is a cloverleaf at the western edge of the course, a highway that allows nature the right-of-way.

Small wonder then that Finns developed *sisu*—the ability to confront adversity with courage, endurance, and tenacity. In athletics, they have left the flash and dash of speed to others, preferring to concentrate on the longer haul. They have dominated Olympic competition in three track-and-field distance events, the 3,000-meter steeplechase, and the 5,000- and 10,000-meter runs. A live legend is Lasse Viren, 5,000- and 10,000-meter champion at both Munich in 1972 and Montreal in 1976, a twin double even the great Nurmi was unable to achieve.

As for the marathon, two Nurmi contemporaries named Hannes Kolehmainen and Albin Stenroos won the Olympic Games of 1920 and 1924. In modern times Finland has managed to produce only a World Championship marathon course, arguably the most beautiful in Europe. This too is an appropriate reflection of the national character: the Finns are known for their strong sense of design.

"I think the Helsinki City Marathon is special because it is so wide open," says Ylonen. "The course is green with birch, pine, and spruce trees, and blue with the water of the Baltic. Here you

MARATHONS

Left: A nation of long distance skiers and runners, Finns are too fit and filled with sisu to give medics much action on raceday.

Facing page, top: Although the seats of Olympic Stadium are empty at the finish, young volunteers stand by to welcome marathoners with oranges, medals, and smiles.

Facing page, bottom: Perhaps Europe's most varied and beautiful marathon course, much of the route blends birch, pine, and spruce trees with Baltic vistas.

feel like you have room to breathe; that you're really free. You can enjoy being in nature, seeing rabbits and birds. Then suddenly you're in the center of the city. The run is not boring at all."

The out-and-back rolling course begins outside Olympic Stadium near the Nurmi statue, winds around the site of the 1952 Games and heads downtown past Finlandia Hall (architect Alvar Aalto's marble masterpiece); the National Museum; and the Parliament Building. Turning west to the waterfront, it traverses the oldest part of city, where farmers once came to pay customs. Next comes an untaxing, northbound trail between sailboats and birches.

Within view of the mansion of former President Urho Kekkonen, the course crosses the first of six bridges that lead to three islands and a peninsula. Along the waterway are embassies, parks, suburbs, forests, office buildings, and a blustery, 2.5-kilometer Baltic seascape. After a circle tour of urban Helsinki—Market Square, South Harbor, Senate Square, and the shopping street Esplanade— the course begins a nearly identical return trip. Only at the 38-kilometer point does it veer up a gradual, one-kilometer hill to proceed along Keskuspuisto Park to the finish line inside the stadium.

Each August, four thousand marathoners race the route of the 1983 World Championships. Since 1981, when the Helsinki City Marathon began, they have been joined annually by at least 100,000 spectators who keep their emotions to themselves. "Finns do not cheer," says Ylonen. "But the runners know they are being supported. Because of Nurmi, distance running is close to the heart of the Finnish people." Sibelius might also have understood the natural sound of silence.

Robert de Castella was triumphant after his 1983 tour of Helsinki in the inaugural World Championships.

HONOLULU, HAWAII

HONOLULU MARATHON

Dr. Jack Scaff, a cardiologist and the spiritual father of the Honolulu Marathon, believes that (a) marathons are for everyone, including heart-attack victims, and (b) they should be entertaining. The result is the ultimate fun run, a blast that begins with a one-hundred-charge fireworks display bursting in the pre-dawn air above Aloha Tower and ends with a 20,000-person picnic in Kapiolani Park. In between is a 26.2-mile stroll through eighty-percent humidity and a matching temperature, weather conditions that also contribute to the race's holiday appeal. "Fear of the heat breeds temperance," says Scaff. Ambition wilts in Honolulu. Good times become more important than fast times for most of the eight thousand runners. One-third of the field spends more than five hours completing the flat, out and mostly back journey along Oahu's beachfront, which is fine by Scaff. The only pace that ever concerned him was a pulsebeat.

In 1973, Scaff decided to train one of his patients at the local YMCA Cardiac Rehabilitation Center to run a marathon, a bold idea. If a person could sustain 120 beats for one hour, he could do it for five, he surmised. He was onto something a little late. Six Toronto heart patients finished the Boston Marathon that year. Scaff

Above: Instead of the usual medals, shell leis await marathoners in Kapiolani Park. Right: Only in Honolulu can a participant run into the dawn.

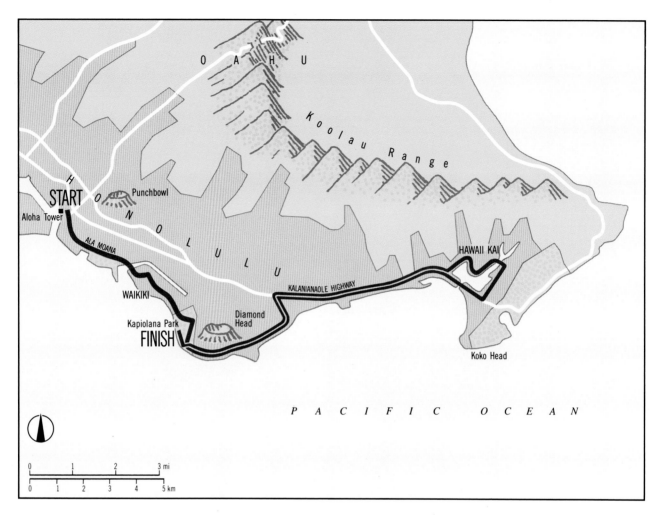

Honolulu Marathon

ORGANIZER *Honolulu Marathon Association*
3435 Waialae Avenue
Room 208
Honolulu, HI 96816
USA
RACE DIRECTOR John Kelleher
DATE Usually the second Sunday in December.
START 6:00 AM at Aloha Tower.
FINISH Kapiolani Park.
TIME LIMIT None.
ELIGIBILITY Open to runners of all abilities.

AWARDS Awards to top finishers in all age groups. Shell leis and T-shirts to all finishers. Official certificate mailed to each finisher.
COURSE RECORDS Ibrahim Hussein, Kenya, 2:12:08 (1985); Patti Catalano, USA, 2:33:24 (1981).

TEMPERATURE 80°F (27°C)
CROWD 50,000
TERRAIN Flat except for short uphill grade on Diamond Head.
COMPETITORS 8,000 from thirty nations.
REFRESHMENTS AND SERVICES Water, cola, and sponges every 2 miles; post-race showers, cola, and massages.

ENTERTAINMENT Fireworks display and military band at the start, hula dancers midway, live rock and Hawaiian music at the finish.
ADDITIONAL EVENTS Runners' mercantile expo and clinics, 4.6-mile Couples Run Thursday morning in Kapiolani Park, Friday evening pasta party, post-race bring-your-own picnic and awards ceremony in Kapiolani Park.
UNUSUAL FEATURE The pre-dawn start.

Parked en route is a luxurious, unofficial water station replete with "butlers" who serve champagne and cake from the boot of a Rolls.

revised his goal, settling for the first American finisher. He went ahead and created a 26.2-mile race in Honolulu, and covered the distance with some 155 others, including Val Nolasco, his runner from the Y. He publicly congratulated Nolasco on the achievement, telling him that he would be an inspiration to thousands of fellow Americans with heart disease. "Val looked embarrassed," recalls Scaff. "Later he quietly told me that he only had a green card, not a US passport. I had trained the first Filipino, as it turned out."

From then on, the Honolulu Marathon stopped taking itself too seriously—a good thing, considering the lighthearted moments that keep cropping up. Some are whimsical. A New Zealander comes to an abrupt stop at the eastern end of the course. He is struck not by the wall, but by the beauty of the Koolau Range. He unslings his camera, aims, and snaps away. After a half-dozen shots, he jogs off to the next photo opportunity. He will take four rolls and seven hours during the event.

Some are fanciful. Richard Field, who runs a Honolulu wine company, creates a lavish, unofficial aid station. Assisted by "butlers" dressed in white tie-and-tails, Field stands by a Rolls-Royce Silver Cloud and serves prune cake and chilled champagne to a privileged few—his friends in the marathon.

Some are alluring. Mindful of a Honolulu Marathon Association suggestion that natives share their Kapiolani picnics with pale off-Island runners, a beautiful Hawaiian girl throws her arms around an untanned stranger and announces, "You're mine!" Lunch, according to legend, lasts three weeks.

Some are musical. Singer Hiromi Go, whose single "Aishu Casablanca" is number one back home, is by far the most famous of the 2,300 Japanese tourists in the race. When he crosses the finish in a

Even a Gurkha, one of the Nepalese soldiers long renowned for toughness, lingers under a cool finish-area shower after battling a hot (80 degree), humid (80 percent) raceday.

respectable 3:38:00, he is still wearing white gloves, his trademark. His appearance is a thriller for two hundred young Japanese spectators who are waiting to cheer their relatives. Rock is thicker than blood. Chorusing his name, the teenagers chase Go and his bodyguards across the park. They reach a parking lot only in time to catch sight of the thirty-year-old idol tossing himself into the back seat of a getaway stretch limo.

Others are literary. Author Hunter S. Thompson arrives on assignment for *Rolling Stone* at a prerace pasta party at Jack Scaff's house. He carries a six-pack of beer and a cigarette, an item that spreads fear and loathing through the living room. Thompson is asked to put out either the cigarette or himself. "He was very good about it," Scaff says. "He went right to the porch."

Scaff leads a training clinic every Sunday from March until marathon week in early December and, to quote the *Star-Bulletin*, "runs the race more religiously than some people brush their teeth." But he resigned the presidency of the HMA a few years ago to launch two shorter events, the Great Aloha and the Jingle Bell Runs, which respectively feature prizes worth $60,000 and fifty singing groups plus, he says, "all kinds of theatrical things."

Gone as well from the Honolulu Marathon are a few Scaff touches: the bugler who called the runners "To the Post" and the hula dancers who shook life into the awards ceremony. But most of the drama remains, including a nature-made spectacle. Daybreak over Diamond Head is a view eclipsing even luminaries like Hiromi Go or frequent entrant Tom Selleck.

Ibrahim Hussein of Kenya holds a stunning course record along with his victory trappings of 1985, when he lowered the previous best time by 3:22.

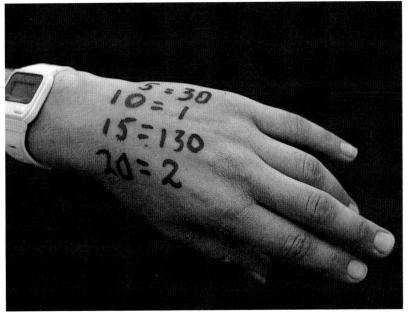

Left: Carla Beurskens fell behind her intended five-mile split times when she was forced to stop at an on-course toilet, but Holland's best marathoner still handily won Honolulu 1985 in 2:35:51.

Facing page, top: The difficult weather conditions and large fields require extended, well staffed water stations, which race founder Jack Scaff claims to be the best anywhere.

Facing page, bottom: Dancing and singing from the sideline on Kalakaua Avenue, Japanese tourists cheer their 2,300 countrymen along Waikiki.

LONDON, ENGLAND

LONDON MARATHON

He felt a bit self-conscious about wearing a USA T-shirt in this, his second London Marathon. The only national team interested in drafting him was the US Army, and that had been years ago in his prime. He was now a middle-aged, middle-of-the-pack tourist from New York. But the touch of vanity—albeit ludicrous—was necessary, he had decided; just the detail to get him through the Isle of Dogs, four and a half depressing miles of vacant docks that weakened the spirit as one approached the wall. Dropping out seemed less possible with the initials of his homeland sewn across his chest.

The T-shirt—along with eight 50-mile training weeks—carried him safely across the only dreary section of the course. He emerged from the Isle of Dogs at the 19.5-mile mark with his nation's honor intact. There was no subsequent collision with the wall, only a close call when a wheelchair grazed his heel. Even the painful cobbles at the Tower of London didn't deter him. After passing Nelson's Column in Trafalgar Square, he entered The Mall. In the distance was Buckingham Palace, to the sides were cheering spectators, and on his scalp were goose bumps.

"Well done, USA!" someone called. The comment was all it took

Good will abounds at the London Marathon, where Good Samaritans gather up the halt and the lame.

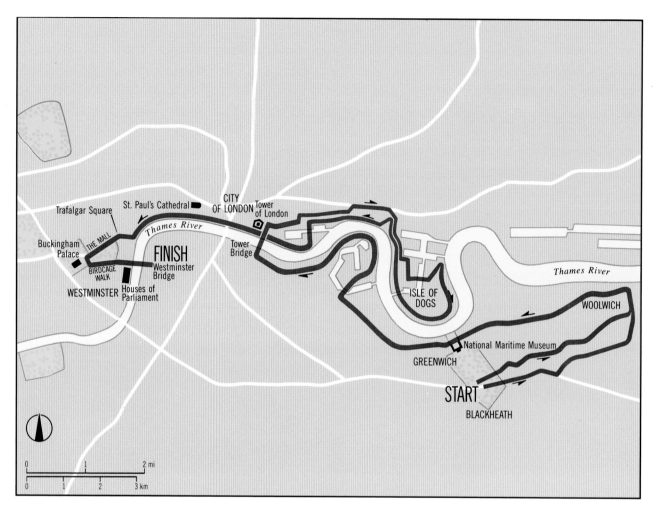

London Marathon

ORGANIZER *London Marathon Limited*
Post Office Box 262
Richmond, Surrey TW10 5JB
England

RACE DIRECTOR Chris Brasher

DATE Usually the second-to-last Sunday in April.

START 9:30 AM at Blackheath and Greenwich Park.

FINISH Westminster Bridge, London.

TIME LIMIT None.

ELIGIBILITY Open to runners of all abilities; runners must be eighteen years old by raceday.

AWARDS Awards to top finishers in all age groups, also several team awards. Medals to all finishers. Results postcard mailed to each finisher.

COURSE RECORDS Steve Jones, Great Britain, 2:08:16 (1985); Ingrid Kristiansen, Norway, 2:21:06 (1985).

TEMPERATURE 50°F (10°C)

CROWD 900,000

TERRAIN Downhill for first 5 miles, flat the rest of the way except for slight rises to Tower Bridge (12.5 miles) and Westminster Bridge.

COMPETITORS 19,000 from forty-seven nations.

REFRESHMENTS AND SERVICES Water every mile, electrolyte drink every other mile; post-race blankets, snack, orange drink.

ENTERTAINMENT Five bands along the way.

ADDITIONAL EVENTS Runners' mercantile expo and clinics, Saturday evening pasta party, awards ceremony.

UNUSUAL FEATURES A crossing of the Eastern and Western Hemispheres at the prime meridian; the best finishing miles in marathoning.

Top: At 6½ miles, the runners detour under the prow of the historic clipper ship Cutty Sark.

to carry reality away. By the time he arrived at the palace and turned left onto Birdcage Walk, he was imagining that he really was an Olympian. The crowd by the Houses of Parliament was cheering only him; the bagpiper stationed at the base of Big Ben squealed news of his arrival; the military band on Westminster Bridge celebrated by striking up the *Chariots of Fire* theme.

Even above the music he could hear the cheers and laughter of the VIP grandstand audience. Laughter? The question popped his fantasy with unnerving suddenness. What's going on? He looked around in time to see an elaborate feathered costume sprint by. As he stared at the receding tail feathers, his legs and arms became unbearably heavy. Even so, he was able to appreciate the joke to the finish. "It's hard to keep on pretending you're Frank Shorter when you've just been passed by someone dressed up as an ostrich," he would often relate. Inside the bird, it turned out, was a TV personality running to raise money for the disabled.

The London race is an annual excuse even for non-celebrities to make fools of themselves for the sake of charities. In return for the pounds–per–mile donations of families and friends, London Marathon entrants have been known to fling dignity aside and parade

Overleaf: The race has worn the sponsoring names of either a razor or a candybar since its start in 1981, but its enduring symbol remains Tower Bridge.

before BBC cameras mass-disguised as the *Let's Make a Deal* studio audience.

Only in London is it possible to see a set of "quintuplets" in giant-size diapers and sunbonnets giving chase to "escaped convicts" in striped prison clothes and toting papier-mâché ball-and-chains. Up ahead, two male marathoners appear as bride and groom. The "newlyweds" share the road with "the suitor," who has arranged for his girlfriend to wait for him at the 23-mile marker. When he arrives, he pulls a rose from his shorts, kneels on the pavement, and proposes. He isn't kidding, it turns out. Sometimes it's difficult to separate the cast from the characters.

Before assuming a fanciful identity of his own, the New Yorker ran across Prince Charles, Mahatma Gandhi, Goofy, and Superman. He also encountered a clarinetist who certainly wasn't Benny Goodman but who still managed a respectable on-the-run rendition of "When the Saints Go Marching In." More impressive was the performance of the real-live race director. En route to a 3:12:00, Chris Brasher stopped off at a pub for a ham sandwich and a pint of beer.

Brasher actually was an Olympic champion. A two-time member of the British team, he won the 3,000-meter steeplechase at the 1956 Games. Another career highlight occurred one spring day in 1954 when he paced Roger Bannister through the first two and a half laps of history's first sub-four-minute mile. In retirement, Brasher popularized the sport of orienteering in England and covered athletics for *The Observer*; but no assignment inspired him quite like his first mass marathon.

"Unlike the Queen in *Through the Looking Glass*, I am not good at believing six impossible things before breakfast," Brasher wrote. "But it was in the small hours of an October morning in 1979 that I had a thought: Last Sunday, during the New York City Marathon, millions of us saw a vision of the human race, happy and united, willing their fellow human beings to a pointless but wonderful victory over mental doubt and body frailty. I wonder whether London could stage such a festival."

Following the advice of the Queen of Hearts, Brasher drew a long breath, shut his eyes, and made the London Marathon an impossibly large success story. Not even he could have foreseen London's 80,000 annual applicants, 23,000 entrants, 19,000 starters, and 18,100 finishers. Among all those nonsensical comic-book characters, March Hares, Dormice, and Mad Hatters were two real-life blonde heroines. Norwegians Grete Waitz and Ingrid Kristiansen raced down the rabbit hole in respective world-record times of 2:25:29 and 2:21:06, the dreamiest numbers of all.

Thousands run for fun, to raise charity money, and to dress up as a convict or gorilla, two of the most popular costumes.

Although under repair in 1985, the world's most famous clock accurately displays the world-record timing of Ingrid Kristiansen's arrival on Westminster Bridge.

MELBOURNE, AUSTRALIA

MELBOURNE MARATHON

For a while, the evidence of global conquest by cheeky Australians was inescapable. Up in the corporate ionosphere flew Rupert Murdoch, lord of the Western presses and newly intent on riding the airwaves of his own US television network. Out to sea sailed *Australia II*, which breezed away with The America's Cup, leaving one of the all-time upsets bobbing in its wake. Across a post-apocalyptic landscape roamed Mad Max, whose movies smashed the notion that adventure mega-hits came only from Hollywood. A true-life road warrior seemed invincible as well, Robert de Castella, winner of marathons at Rotterdam, Fukuoka, the Brisbane Commonwealth Games, and the Helsinki World Championships. Australia was on a tear.

It could not last, of course. Murdoch became a United States citizen. American companies threw millions at several Cup challengers, whatever it took to rock the boat. *Mad Max*'s makers greedily invited Tina Turner to share the credits. And, although the Olympic favorite de Castella finished out of the medals in Los Angeles, no one remained more admired by his countrymen than the Melbourne runner. In Australia, a sports-crazed nation of only fifteen million inhabitants, a world title is regarded as the most

The field hospital beyond the finish line has a staff of fifteen, and forty-five more medics are along the course.

precious achievement of all. De Castella had managed one, and was considered still young enough for more, perhaps even at the 1988 Seoul Olympic Games.

Optimism is as commonplace in Australia as a can of Foster's beer, and bubbles to the surface just as readily. Ask an Aussie what his two-hundred-year-old country is likely to become once it really gets rolling—in the mid-twenty-first century, say—and a one-word answer comes back: superpower. At the moment, Australians happily settle for the small potatoes—delighting in an MP who disrupted Parliament by dressing up as a chicken and making barnyard noises during a debate ("It can't be a member of the opposition," announced one eyewitness. "It has a head."), rooting for a cricket victory, at least over New Zealand, and emulating a celebrity by running a marathon or two. De Castella did not exactly inspire a seismic boom that shook golf clubs, racing forms, tennis rackets, surfboards, and sailing tillers from the collective grasp. But there was indeed a noticeable *pop!*—especially in de Castella's home-town.

The Melbourne Marathon swelled to 6,900 in 1983, an increase of 1,600 entries. "De Castella became a bit of a hero that year," says Ted Paulin, the race's executive director. "His success gave our race a nice lift." Both man and marathon peaked simultaneously, as it turned out. The faddish runners, Deeks' Freaks, have drifted off, leaving five thousand marathoners from five Australian states and twelve countries to enjoy the October event that lives up to its

The route is scenic all along Port Phillip Bay, especially on Beach Road, in towns such as Mentone.

Mindful of relatives' long, anxious wait for marathoners to finish, the Melbourne City Council presents some tall distractions at the family festival in Alexandra Gardens.

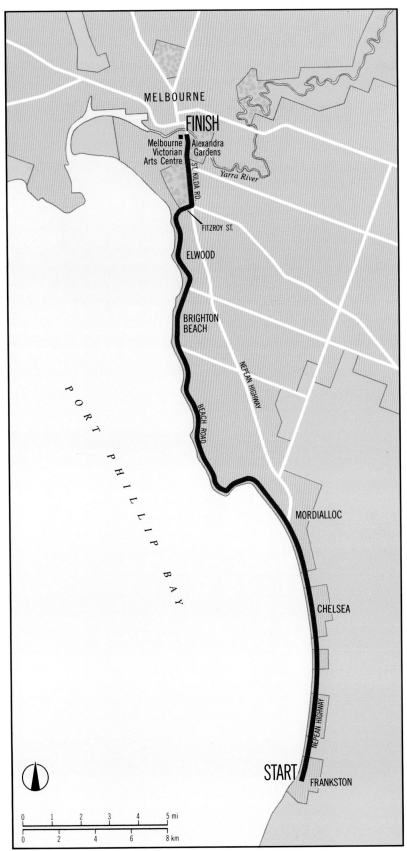

Melbourne Marathon

ORGANIZER *Melbourne Marathon Inc.*
Vicsport Centre Olympic Park
Swan Street
Melbourne, Victoria 3002
Australia

RACE DIRECTOR Ted Paulin
DATE Second Sunday in October.
START 8:00 AM at Frankston.
FINISH Melbourne Victorian Arts Centre.
TIME LIMIT Six hours.
ELIGIBILITY Open to runners of all abilities; runners must be eighteen years old by raceday.

AWARDS Awards to top finishers in all age groups, also awards to top teams and local runners. Medals to all finishers. Official certificate, badge, and results magazine mailed to each finisher.
COURSE RECORDS Bill Rodgers, USA, 2:11:08 (1982); Rhonda Mallinder, Australia, 2:37:56 (1983).

TEMPERATURE 65°F (18°C)
CROWD 150,000
TERRAIN Flat except for three hills located between 17 and 21 kilometers and an 800-meter climb up Fitzroy Street at 37 kilometers.
COMPETITORS 5,000 from twelve nations.
REFRESHMENTS AND SERVICES Water and sponges every 5 kilometers; post-race massages, hot tubs.

ENTERTAINMENT A celebrity starter; clowns, bands, and buy-your-own picnics at the finish.
ADDITIONAL EVENTS Friday evening pasta party, awards ceremony on raceday that is continued at an awards party one month later.
UNUSUAL FEATURE The post-race family festival.

slogan, the Top Run Down Under.

Few marathons are as image-minded as Melbourne. The concept was hatched by Peter Clemenger, managing director of one of Melbourne's top advertising agencies, during a business trip to New York. He chanced upon the New York City Marathon and was impressed enough to dash off a letter to Brian Dixon, Victoria's Minister for Youth, Sport, and Recreation, suggesting a similar mass marathon at home. A few phone calls later, the 1978 race was well on the way. Things happen fast in Australia, even collecting a sponsor. The Victorian Dairy Industry Authority was introducing a line of flavored milk called Big M to pep up a sagging market, and eagerly dropped 100,000 Australian dollars into the bucket. Milk and marathon made music, the milk executives decided. Healthy, wholesome, and thirsty bodies would naturally lap up banana and chockberry Big Ms as they jogged the All-Australian scenery of Port Phillip Bay from Frankston to Melbourne. "I had to tell them that runners wouldn't want to be scoffing down milk," says Paulin, a former ad salesman and seven-time professional marathon champion. "That detail didn't bother them at all."

Paulin and his organizing committee developed their own sales

At the end comes a rush of accomplishment, as demonstrated by John Brennan of Melbourne's Malvern Athletic Club, who joyously completes the 1985 race in 2:26:56.

The best recovery area in mass marathoning is at the Top Run Down Under, where even average battlers can enjoy a post-race soak in a hot tub.

strategy over the years. "We do everything we can think of to make the average battler feel important," he says. Melbourne's participants receive a train trip to the start, a medal at the finish, plus a certificate, an "I finished" sew-on patch, and a results magazine in the mail. On-course gifts are the cheers of 150,000 Aussies, the beautiful bay shores between Mordialloc and Brighton Beach, and the renowned topless sands of Elwood. The tree-lined boulevard of St. Kilda Road grandly concludes the route beneath the spire of the city's new Victorian Arts Centre.

The recovery area in the Alexandra Gardens is special too, a comfortable respite from the three half-way hills along Beach Road and the nasty climb at 37 kilometers on Fitzroy Street. Here are hot tubs to soak in, soft grass to lie down on, and a massage tent to repair to. Patient family and friends also have plenty of diversions: a couple on stilts, the Lord Mayor in his robes, a history-of-the-marathon exhibit, country and jazz bands, and picnic lunches.

Only the national hero himself is missing, always off making his living in rich races like the America's Marathon/Chicago. But there is another de Castella in the field to proudly point out. His name is Rolet. He is Robert's father, a battler like the rest of us.

Big M Girls, wholesome representatives of the sponsoring milk company, greeted finishers with medals and kisses until 1986, when Budget Rent A Car took to the roadrace.

Left: One year after being beaten only by national hero Robert de Castella at the 1982 Brisbane Commonwealth Games, Tanzanian Juma Ikangaa returned to Australia to win the first of two straight Melbournes.

MONTREAL, CANADA

MONTREAL INTERNATIONAL MARATHON

Surrounded by the St. Lawrence River and sprawled at the foot of Mount Royal, Montreal remains sheltered from urban blight. No graffiti scar the monuments in the old city. No drug pushers lurk beside the ponds of Lafontaine Park. No uniformed guards patrol the galleries of the Museum of Fine Art, not even when a Picasso exhibit hangs there. No angry car horns jam away at rush-hour traffic on Sherbrooke Street. The only urban crisis is one of identity.

Claimed by the French, taken by the Americans, and conquered by the British, the local ego has been jerked around right through modern times, when Quebec has tried to gain independence from Canada. As the standard definition goes, a French Canadian is a Frenchman who lives like an American under a British form of government. "Quebec is unique," insists Serge Arsenault, president and director general of the Montreal International Marathon. "We are six million French people in the middle of 250 million English-speaking people with a different culture. Because of this, we are used to cheering others." He knows all about that. A sportscaster for the Canadian Broadcasting Corporation, he spends many workdays

Ten thousand starters, the fifth largest marathon field, await the cannon blast that will start them across the St. Lawrence River via the Jacques-Cartier Bridge.

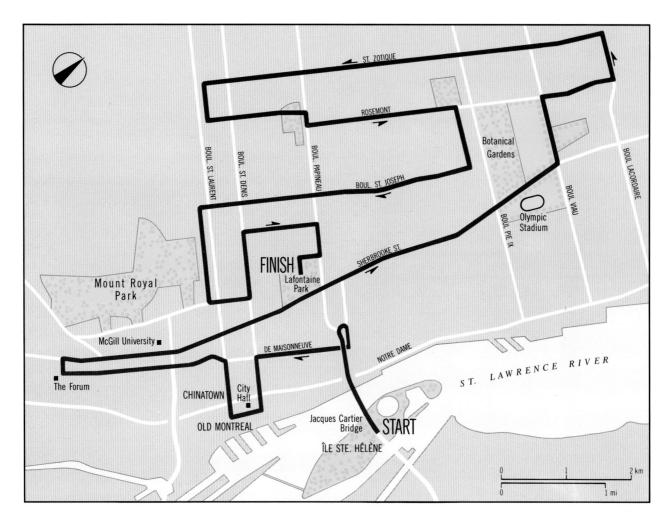

Montreal International Marathon

ORGANIZER *Montreal International
Marathon
Post Office Box 1570
Station B
Montreal H3B 3L2, Quebec
Canada*
RACE DIRECTOR Serge Arsenault
DATE The fourth Sunday in September.
START 9:10 AM on the Jacques-Cartier
Bridge.
FINISH Lafontaine Park.
TIME LIMIT Six hours.
ELIGIBILITY Open to runners of all abilities; runners must be sixteen years old
by raceday.

AWARDS Awards to top finishers in all age
groups. Medals to all finishers. Official
certificate and results magazine mailed to
each finisher.
COURSE RECORDS Kebede Balcha, Ethiopia, 2:10:03 (1983); Françoise Bonnet,

France, 2:33:44 (1985).

TEMPERATURE 65°F (18°C)
CROWD 400,000
TERRAIN Flat after the bridge except for
gradual inclines on Sherbrooke (between
11 and 12 kilometers) and Lacordaire
(between 19 and 20 kilometers).
COMPETITORS 10,000 from twenty nations.
REFRESHMENTS AND SERVICES Water every
2 kilometers from the 4th to the 40th
kilometer points, electrolyte drink every
4 kilometers from the 6th to the 30th
kilometer points, sponges every 6 kilometers beginning at the 16-kilometer
point; post-race blankets, cheese, yogurt,
fruit, beer, massages.

ADDITIONAL EVENTS Runners' mercantile
expo, clinics, awards ceremony, post-race
party for volunteers.

describing the play of the Americans who fill the baseball roster of the Montreal Expos.

The idea for a hometown marathon struck Arsenault in 1977 while on assignment overseas, covering the first International Amateur Athletic Federation World Cup in Düsseldorf, Germany. "I was surprised that the competition did not include a marathon," he says. "I was a fun runner back then and had finished three marathons, including New York. I complained on the air. An official sarcastically said to me, 'The next World Cup is in Montreal in 1979. If you are so interested, you should organize a marathon there.' So that is what I did."

One Sunday each September, 10,000 runners assemble on the Jacques-Cartier Bridge and follow a cannon blast across the river. After passing the towering Radio-Canada Building, they invade Old Montreal, site of the 1642 settlement of Ville Marie. One landmark

The vivid green and red colors of Ethiopia traditionally fly at the front at Montreal, a race won by Kebede Balcha more often than not.

is City Hall, where history was made as recently as 1967 when Charles de Gaulle stood on the balcony and fueled the separatist movement by shouting, *"Vive le Québec libre!"* Runners abruptly shift accents in Chinatown, a neighborhood lean on length but stuffed with eateries. Civic pride dwells up the road at the corner of de Maisonneuve and Closse, address of the Forum and the Montreal Canadiens, hockey's most successful team.

The course hitches Sherbrooke crosstown, taking in the art museum, the Ritz-Carlton Hotel, McGill University, the Montreal Library, the Botanical Gardens, and Olympic Stadium, which looks like an immense, grounded flying saucer. Beyond the stacked-domino-shaped 1976 Olympic Village and a nine-hole golf course, the route becomes residential along the eastern edge of the city. Near the midway point, the sights run out and the crowds take over. Apart from occasional views of Mount Royal and a one-kilometer peek at the outdoor cafés of St-Denis Street, the second-half scenery is row housing.

"We used to end the race at Expo 67 on Ile Sainte-Hélène," Arsenault says. "The last eight kilometers were very pretty but very empty. We redesigned the course to follow the population curve to a new midtown finish in Lafontaine Park. Now we have a good crowd, the runner's fuel. When he is tired, the marathoner needs people, not postcards." Lining the way home are 200,000 spectators who belt out high-pitched cheers at the inevitable foreign leader, often Ethiopia's Kebede Balcha, winner of four of the first seven races.

Arsenault annually imports sixty to eighty athletes from nearly twenty national teams, but he is mindful of the rest of the field as well. Entrants are treated to slick training guides; aid stations every two kilometers stocked with 600,000 bottles of Evian water; gold, silver, and bronze time-based medals; a six-hundred-bed hospital tent staffed by one hundred medical professionals; post-race snack packs filled with yogurt, cheese, and four varieties of fruit. "We charge a $10 entry fee, but each runner costs us $160," says Arsenault.

Because his name was well known from television, Arsenault attracted sponsors from the start. With a direct-expense budget of 1.6 million Canadian dollars in hand, his only struggle was with himself. "I was very tempted to go commercial; to try and buy superstars with masses of appearance money," he says. "One year I *did* pay. Many runners no one heard of finished before my guy, who coasted in with a smile. After that, I decided to be content with one goal: to try to have Montreal recognized as the best-organized marathon in the world." That would be identity enough.

Both highly trained and accomplished athletes, a runner and a wheelchair racer share a lonely stretch of the mostly flat, fast course.

MOSCOW, USSR

MOSCOW INTERNATIONAL PEACE MARATHON

The Moscow Marathon parades vivid images past the eye: a lipstick-red portrait of Lenin looming three stories above the pavement; St. Basil's Cathedral floating beyond a sea of silver tour buses, its billowed cupolas splashed with color; bikini-clad teenagers in Gorky Park soaking the runners with plastic bags full of water toted from the Moscow River by their boyfriends; a post-finish encounter with a Russian marathoner whose outstretched hand is offering not congratulations, but rubles for a pair of American-made running shoes.

The most enduring sight, though, is the military presence. Spaced every 30 yards along the course are soldiers wearing brown uniforms and stone faces. Many hold ropes waist-high to prevent spectators from spilling onto the roadway, an absurd detail. Except for the three-mile stretch in the park, there is no crowd to control.

Regrettably for the five thousand runners who take part in the grandly named Moscow International Peace Marathon, the USSR's biggest, most prestigious marathon, many midtowners flee to their country dachas on summer weekends. The rest choose not to spend a dogday afternoon hovering on sidewalks baked by the afternoon sun, even when the dates are scheduled to coincide with such

The military mans the water and sponge stations and accounts for nearly all of the spectators. Right: Viewed from each side of the Moscow River, the Kremlin is a dominant landmark passed by marathoners four times.

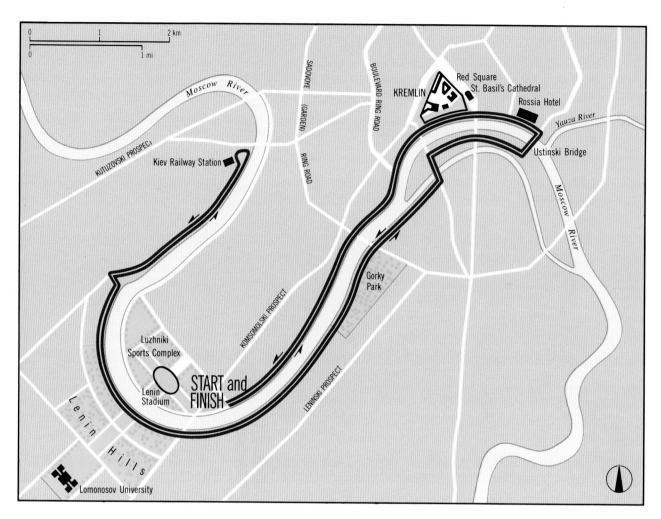

Moscow International Peace Marathon

ORGANIZER *Moscow Sports Committee*
Marhlevskava 18
Moscow
USSR
RACE DIRECTOR A. N. Kovalev
DATE Second Saturday in August.
START 4:00 PM at the Luzhniki Sports
Complex.
FINISH Luzhniki Sports Complex.
TIME LIMIT Five hours.
ELIGIBILITY Open to runners of all abilities; runners must be sixteen years old
by raceday.

AWARDS Awards to top finishers in all age
groups. Medals and official certificates to
all finishers.
COURSE RECORDS Waldemar Cierpinski,
East Germany, 2:11:03 (1980); Nadezhda
Gumerova, USSR, 2:33:35 (1986).

TEMPERATURE 80°F (27°C)
CROWD 5,000
TERRAIN Flat except for the ramps of two
bridges.
COMPETITORS 5,000 from fourteen nations.
REFRESHMENTS AND SERVICES Water,
juice, and tea every 5 kilometers;
sponges midway between water stations;
post-race sports drink.

ENTERTAINMENT None.
ADDITIONAL EVENTS Simultaneous 10-
kilometer race from Luzhniki Sports
Complex to the Kremlin and back,
awards ceremony the day after the marathon.
UNUSUAL FEATURE The ever-present military.

crowd-pleasers as The Day of the Sportsman, a national celebration of athletics, and the Goodwill Games.

One raceday, a heat wave drove the temperature to 95 degrees, 15 degrees above the norm, causing half the field to withdraw. Remaining mostly at the rear of the scorched pack that year were three hundred visitors from thirteen foreign countries—twelve according to *Pravda*. No mention was made of the forty participating Americans because, one Intourist guide obliquely explained, "on the anniversary of the Hiroshima bombing it is inappropriate to report that Japanese and Americans are running together."

If the hardy traveler is willing to be overlooked by the press,

Elite athletes were invited to road test the Olympic course in 1979, but it would be another three years before the Moscow Sports Committee allowed the same run for everyone.

overexposed to the sun, overcome by loneliness, and overprotected by the Army, the Moscow Marathon provides a thrill. This isn't any old stroll around the block, after all, but a run through the capital of the hostile adversary, a locale to inspire patriotic effort. Dropping out is unthinkable and unnecessary, thanks to aid stations serving apricot juice, hot tea, boiled water, and cold sponges.

The course is special too. It follows the footsteps of the 1980 Olympians, although in some years the finish has been moved outside Lenin Stadium to a less dramatic conclusion in a parking lot of the Luzhniki Sports Complex. The flat, out-and-back route winds entirely along the Moscow River through a brighter city than one expects—white, yellow, and pale blue architecture blooms among the gray Stalin-era hulks. After passing before the Kremlin Wall, the St. Basil's side of Red Square, and the Rossia Hotel, the course bridges the river and curves toward Gorky Park, festive site of amusement rides and public bathing areas. The turnaround comes beyond the Kiev Railway Station, at the end of a two-mile stretch of highway, the marathon's only depressing tract.

Forty-two-kilometer races for elite runners have been held in the city since the 1930s, but only after the Moscow Olympic Games did the local sports authorities decide to give the long run to everyone. "Running had come into fashion," says Vladimir Geshkin, foreign editor of *Sovietski Sport.* "Suddenly many people were running in the summertime to stay in good health for cross-country skiing. We knew how to put on 80-kilometer races with 20,000 skiers. But making a race for thousands of runners in hot weather was something we had to learn about."

The Moscow Sports Committee invited Fred Lebow, president of the New York Road Runners Club, to Moscow in 1982. In return, Lebow was promised that three top Soviet women would compete in his New York City Marathon. The exchange of athletes for expertise was a rare example of post-boycott détente, indicating Moscow's determination to produce its own first-class marathon. The goal was quickly achieved by copying New York's organizational chart, including the unnecessary number of security personnel placed en route.

Attendance is likely to improve due to government policy. The Kremlin has ordered in a fitness boom as an antidote to alcoholism. One hour of exercise daily is the recommended adult dosage. "Plants and factories are urged to spend three percent of their profits on health facilities for their workers," says Geshkin, who then adds another reason why running may soon appeal to the masses. "Mr. Gorbachev likes to jog."

Even though raceday 1985 was Moscow's hottest in a century, ample doses of water every 2½ kilometers enabled each of the 2,500 entrants to safely survive the 95 degree temperature.

Facing page, top: A contingent representing Italy poses in Red Square before boarding a bus to the start.

Facing page, bottom: Wisely shaded from the August afternoon sun, runners from fourteen nations begin their journey in the parking lot of the Luzhniki Sports Complex, an indoor arena built for the 1980 Games.

NEW YORK CITY MARATHON

The New York City Marathon is a people festival more than a race; it's a multicultural journey past Hispanic kids on Brooklyn's Fourth Avenue hoping for high-fives, Hasidic Jews in Williamsburg offering orange slices, East Side yuppies jammed four-deep before the First Avenue singles bars craning for glimpses of friends, a black high-school band in Harlem driving runners through the wall with four straight hours of the theme from *Rocky*, and anxious relatives in Central Park tossing encouragement to strangers as they wait. At the center of attention are the runners, some of whom come dressed as clowns, jesters, Superheroes, and a menagerie of beasts and birds. They come as themselves too, from fifty states and seventy countries.

New York has become the state-of-the-sport model of how to send thousands of runners safely through inner cities. Dedicated to serving all its people as well as the elite athletes, this was the event that introduced automated number bibs, bar codes, computer timing, and pasta parties. But mostly, it brought out the people, showing the world that the marathon wasn't restricted to cardiovascular marvels who trained 120 miles each week.

"I knew the marathon would appeal to the average runner be-

Above: Fred Lebow, marathoning's principal popularizer, has completed some seventy marathons in twenty-five nations and has a personal best of 3:29:00. Right: Raceday 1985 was a steamy 75 degrees.

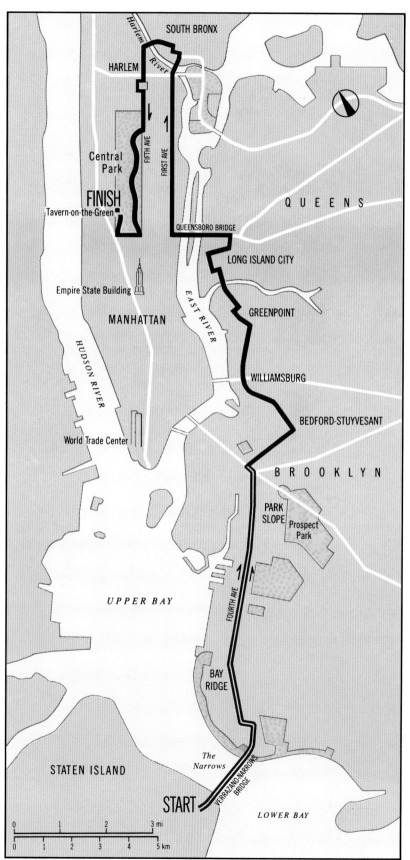

New York City Marathon

ORGANIZER *New York Road Runners Club*
International Running Center
9 East 89th Street
New York, NY 10128
USA
RACE DIRECTOR Fred Lebow
DATE Last Sunday in October or the first
Sunday in November.
START 10:45 AM on the Verrazano-Narrows Bridge.
FINISH Tavern-on-the-Green restaurant,
Central Park.
TIME LIMIT None.
ELIGIBILITY Open to runners of all abilities; runners must be sixteen years old
by raceday.

AWARDS Awards to top finishers in all age
groups, also awards to top teams and
local runners. Medals to all finishers;
roses to women finishers. Results postcard and official certificate mailed to
each finisher.
COURSE RECORDS Alberto Salazar, USA,
2:08:13 (1981); Allison Roe, New Zealand, 2:25:29 (1981).

TEMPERATURE 60°F (15°C)
CROWD 1 million
TERRAIN A mile climb up the Verrazano-Narrows Bridge at the start, a ¾-mile
climb up the Queensboro Bridge (14.5
miles), and three short hills in Central
Park (22.5 miles, 24.5 miles, and the
finish).
COMPETITORS 19,000 from seventy nations.
REFRESHMENTS AND SERVICES Water every
mile, electrolyte drink every other mile;
post-race blankets, snacks, mineral
water, and massages.

ENTERTAINMENT Six bands along the way.
ADDITIONAL EVENTS Runners' mercantile
expo and clinics, 2-mile, Saturday morning International Breakfast Run for foreign entrants from the United Nations to
Tavern-on-the-Green, Saturday evening
pasta party, awards ceremony, disco
party.
UNUSUAL FEATURES The most dramatic
start in marathoning; international flavor;
and the seven-figure crowd.

cause I was one myself," says race director Fred Lebow. Sometimes genius sounds so simple.

Since 1970, when he put up nearly one thousand dollars of his own money and sent 126 runners looping Central Park, the race has belonged to Lebow more than anyone, even habitual winner Grete Waitz. By now, all of New York must know that Lebow soared out of the Transylvanian darkness and nested in Manhattan's garment district. He began running to improve his tennis, and became so entranced by the activity that he quit his job and lost his girlfriend. He took over the one-room, West Side YMCA headquarters of the New York Road Runners Club and launched the marathon that eventually became road racing's equivalent of Woodstock.

Lebow's decision to lift the 1976 race from its pastoral setting and roll it into all five city boroughs was not only inspired, it was perfectly timed. The event was embraced by New Yorkers; here was something good happening in their near-bankrupt land of grime and crime. Two thousand people voluntarily ran from Staten Island, across Brooklyn and Queens, up Manhattan to the Bronx, and back through Harlem to Central Park. Nobody had been killed, raped, mugged, or spray-painted; instead they had been applauded, even cheered. The marathon was evidence of a city pulling hard for itself. New York suddenly had a pat on its back and a hit on its hands.

Those first footsteps along the Verrazano-Narrows Bridge were also clues that a running boom was about to thunder across America. Five thousand runners assembled on the bridge the following year, including author Jim Fixx, who was celebrating the publication date of *The Complete Book of Running*. Although his book would become a phenomenal bestseller, Fixx believed Lebow to be the sport's true popularizer.

The Grete Waitz victory wave, demonstrated here in 1985 for the seventh time in eight years, has become a traditional concluding gesture in Central Park.

Focusing on the experience, an entrant records the sights along her five-borough, all-around-the-town tour.

"That was Fred Lebow's contribution," Fixx told interviewer Richard Woodley eight days before his fatal heart attack. "I think he had a vision—I don't know where he got it—that running could or should be adapted to participation by masses of people. Maybe more than anybody else, he helped make it that way. Primarily with his New York City Marathon . . . It was such a magnet to people's imaginations, a wonderful, thrilling affair for the mass of runners . . . and spectators."

The numbers grew bigger each year. Lebow now accepts nearly half of the marathon's 40,000 applicants, who are supported by seven thousand volunteers, a $2.5 million budget, $275,000 in prize money, and one million onlookers. He also enlarged his office space, moving the NYRRC out of the Y and into a town house off Fifth Avenue, which he named the International Running Center. He became notorious enough to be called an egomaniac, tsar, tyrant, and the most innovative and influential of the world's race directors.

Lebow even managed to attract television's big eye, convincing ABC that Americans would spend a Sunday morning in the fall watching people they have never heard of sweat for three live hours. Among the telecast's memorable moments—the epic Verrazano start, the welcoming crowds on First Avenue, the agonizing struggle over the hills of Central Park—there is the dance of a bearded, hawk-nosed man in a billed cap who hops the winners home to the finish. Who can begrudge Lebow a few annual, highly visible jumps for joy?

With a fireboat below and balloons, blimp and helicopters overhead, the epic start across the Verrazano-Narrows Bridge is so exciting most marathoners don't notice that the first mile is entirely uphill.

Above: Race Director Lebow lends a shoulder to Alberto Salazar in 1982, guiding his three-time winner to a television interview.

PARIS, FRANCE

PARIS MARATHON

After five major route changes in seven years, organizers of the Paris Marathon finally chose to follow the sensible course of the Seine.

The time-filling yo-yo exhibition by Team Coca-Cola long over, the grandstand crowd is now being entertained by the real thing—a stream of marathoners slogging through a May rain to the finish on Avenue Foch. The mayor of the city departs after presenting trophies to the male and wheelchair winners, and even the attention of the race announcer wanders off the job. He is distracted by angry journalists who encircle a race official to complain that the press bus had twice been ordered off the course by traffic police. The official shrugs. What can he do, the gesture seems to say. Voices are raised in frustration and fingers jab the damp air.

The argument stops when someone in the stands shouts the arrival of the first female. Eyes scan the avenue and settle on a woman running along with a grin and a cast. The journalists will soon learn that she is a phys-ed teacher from Manchester, England, who broke her arm spotting a student vaulter, that she trained all winter on an exercise bike, and that she entered France without a passport. But at the moment they are hopeful only of hearing her name, which fails to arrive on time by loudspeaker.

The announcer discovers that he has misplaced his entry list. He

jumps off his platform, snatches a program from a startled spectator, scurries back to his perch, and riffles the pages. *"La première femme, Maureen Hurst!"* he breathlessly calls some moments after she has anonymously crossed the line.

It is surprising that the announcer did not knock over his microphone and crash in a heap, given the slapstick nature of the event. Along with the spectacular scenery of the banks of the Seine, the Paris Marathon is also notable for such slip-ups as:

The plain, white T-shirt. The rumored reasons vary—an organizer was ill; the manufacturer was on strike; a bill was not paid—but one year many entrants received unmarked articles of clothing as race mementos.

The long, limp line. When Paris instituted a pasta party, hundreds of diners, and only one spaghetti server, showed up. "I can't believe I waited forty minutes for food I don't even like," marveled one of the carbo-loaders the day after.

The bureaucratic party-pooper. Just when the race had been properly established as a Saturday-night spectacle, the Prefecture of Police decided it was a traffic hazard and imposed a return of the racedate to Sunday morning, thereby eliminating the crowd along with the cars.

The paging-Inspector-Clouseau episode. Mystery clouds one paragraph of the authorized race history: "An enormous upset in the women's competition with the victory of an unknown Jacqueline Courtade in 2:58:14. Having never before been credited with such a performance, this laureate for a day would never again appear in the record books. This situation places the authenticity of the results obtained by Jacqueline Courtade on this May 14th, 1983 under suspicion. With no formal proof of foul play, we will leave her the benefit of the doubt."

The magic forest. Without bar codes on number bibs, the computerized surveillance system used by most mass marathons, Paris invites cheating. "So many people were waiting to jump into the race in the Bois de Boulogne that it looked like the trees were wearing numbers," said a member of the honest majority of the 15,000 entrants in 1984. The following year, two tardy Parisians were less inhibited about cutting the first few kilometers from the course. They parked en route, threw their street clothes into the trunk, and began running.

The close calls. The outcome of two races were affected by—to borrow the printed words of the Paris Marathon Association—"the indescribable mess caused by the well-known lack of discipline of Paris motorists." American Ron Tabb lost his concentration and the

Facing page: Crossing Le Pont d'Iéna in the shadow of the Eiffel Tower, even a mass marathon field is diminished by Paris' monumental grandeur.

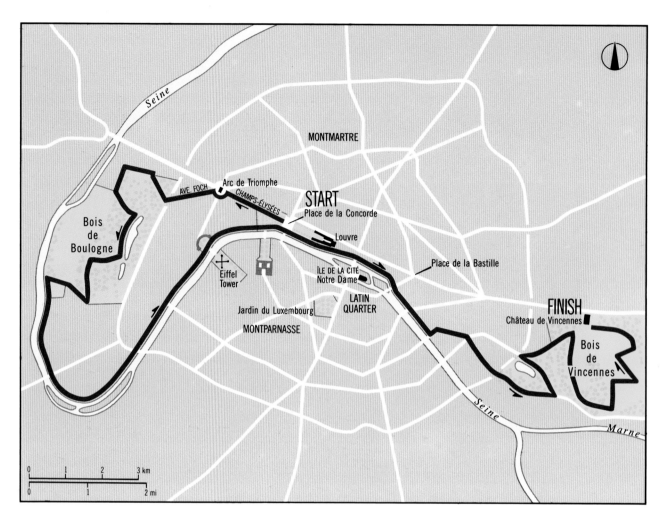

Paris Marathon

ORGANIZER *Sports International Organization S.A.*
59 Avenue Victor Hugo
92100 Boulogne
France
RACE DIRECTOR Raymond Lorre
DATE First or second Sunday in May.
START 10:30 AM at Place de la Concorde.
FINISH Château de Vincennes.
TIME LIMIT None.
ELIGIBILITY Open to runners of all abilities.

AWARDS Awards to top finishers in all age groups. Medals to all finishers. Official certificate mailed to each finisher.
RACE RECORDS Jacky Boxberger, France, 2:10:49 (1985); Maria Lalut, France, 2:32:16 (1986).

TEMPERATURE 65°F (18°C)
CROWD 100,000
TERRAIN Flat except for gradual uphills for the first 2 kilometers, 5 to 8 kilometers, 30 to 32 kilometers, and 35 to 37 kilometers.
COMPETITORS 9,000 from twenty nations.
REFRESHMENTS AND SERVICES Water, sports drink, and oranges every 5 kilometers; post-race blankets, apples, oranges, yogurt, cookies, juice.

ENTERTAINMENT Four bands along the way.
ADDITIONAL EVENTS Saturday evening pasta party, awards ceremony.
UNUSUAL FEATURE Springtime in Paris.

lead in 1981 after he was nearly struck by an automobile. Three races later, France's Jacky Boxberger was hampered by a swerving motorbike 500 meters from the end. He finished one second behind the winner, Djiboutian Ahmed Saleh.

The all-city tour. Perhaps inspired by the New York City Marathon's five-borough course, Race Director Raymond Lorre took the four-year-old Paris Marathon out of the Bois in 1979 and rerouted it past all but one of the city's twenty-two districts. The innovation added five thousand runners, a half-million spectators, twenty-one town halls, and far too many hills. That course was "hellish," "terribly difficult," and dotted with "very hard climbs," PMA literature confessed. It was dropped in favor of a saner approach by the Seine.

Educated by a decade of pratfalls, the PMA has removed most of the bugs and nearly all of the hills. The Paris Marathon is at last worthy of its setting.

Gone is the wild and wet raceday when the assembled field was kept in check by fire hoses, but the 9,000 starters are still in for a blast—a well run tour of Paris in springtime.

REYKJAVIK, ICELAND

REYKJAVIK MARATHON

I celand remains geologically immature, an oddity of fire and ice. Glaciers cover eleven percent of the island. The rest is largely an expanding lava field potholed with geysers. Since its settlement in the ninth century, Iceland's frequent volcanic eruptions have destroyed half the vegetation, leaving the sheep and ponies room to roam over only twenty-five percent of the land mass.

The people have understandably taken off to the sea, notably Leif Ericsson, who found fame and the North American continent five hundred years before Columbus did. Iceland has helped to launch other adventurers as well, both real and imaginary. Jules Verne chose Snaefellsjokull Glacier for the beginning of *The Journey to the Center of the Earth*. NASA selected the Askja Volcano area as a suitable training site for its moon-bound Apollo astronauts. The reclusive Bobby Fischer agreed to Reykjavik as an acceptably remote European location for his chess battle with Boris Spassky.

Apart from sport fisherman (Iceland's salmon rivers are among the world's best), vacationers are not easily lured to this barren place where beer is banned, the TV station takes Thursdays off the air, and hot times are spent lolling in a thermal spring or browsing for just the right sweater. In such a locale, travel agents aren't made.

Several hundred entrants in the half-marathon and seven-kilometer fun run accompany the 120 marathoners past the earth-colored buildings of the Reykjavik central city to begin the day's events.

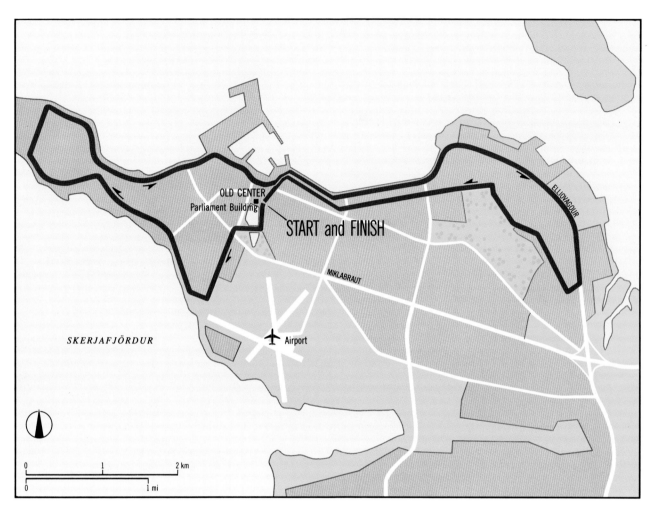

Reykjavik Marathon

ORGANIZER *Reykjavik Marathon*
13 Posthusstraeti
101 Reykjavik
Iceland
RACE DIRECTOR Knutur Oskarsson
DATE Fourth Sunday in August.
START 12:00 noon by Loekjargata, Old Centre.
FINISH By Loekjargata, Old Centre.
TIME LIMIT None.
ELIGIBILITY Open to runners of all abilities; runners must be sixteen years old by raceday.

AWARDS Awards to top finishers in all age groups. Medals to all finishers.
COURSE RECORDS Boudjenane Chaibi, France, 2:20:30 (1986); Leslie Watson, Great Britain, 2:52:45 (1985).

TEMPERATURE 50°F (10°C)
CROWD 1,000
TERRAIN Completely flat.
COMPETITORS 120 from thirteen nations.
REFRESHMENTS AND SERVICES Water and sports drink every 5 kilometers; post-race blankets, sports drink, juice, soup.

ENTERTAINMENT A band at the start.
ADDITIONAL EVENTS Saturday evening pasta party, simultaneous half-marathon and 7-kilometer fun run, awards ceremony, gala dinner, disco party.
UNUSUAL FEATURES Perhaps the most charming of all the world's marathons; certainly the least polluted of all capital-city marathons.

"I was born into the business," explains Knutur Oskarsson, who managed to keep his optimism as director of Urval Travel. "I was always looking for ideas to extend our tourist season. One day in 1982, I arrived in Göteborg, Sweden on business and came upon thousands of people. I didn't know what was happening. I was told that they were all waiting to see a running race with Grete Waitz. I started to read the papers, and learned that this sort of thing was happening in every town in Europe. This is a great idea, I thought."

Oskarsson flew the concept back to Reykjavik, the most northern capital in the world and home to 90,000 of Iceland's 250,000 residents, nearly all of whom believed that running was best left to the quadrupeds. "A psychiatrist friend of mine was a jogger," says Oskarsson. "People thought he was crazy. Sometimes stones were thrown at him. Another Icelander got the running habit while working in the United States. Back for a vacation, he went for a winter run all bundled up. An old lady saw him and called the police. He was picked up."

The foremost task was clearly educational, Oskarsson knew. He decided not only to stage an international marathon but to simultaneously include two shorter races as well, a half-marathon and a seven-kilometer fun run. "We knew we had to create local interest

Unaccustomed to traveling long distances on land, Icelanders leave foreigners alone to cheer their annual marathon and wave the colors of a country one of their own discovered.

A corporate team evidences the successful takeoff of an idea intended to lift the late-summer tourist season.

by getting people to take part," he says.

Held in late August of 1984, the first Reykjavik Marathon appealed to only twenty runners, but two hundred others also reached the pretty finish near a swan lake in the city's Old Centre. One year later, the three-event field more than doubled. Oskarsson has established a good deal more than local awareness of long-distance running: Reykjavik is as charming as any marathon in the world.

Where else can a marathoner start out running with excited children? Of all the city marathons, only here is one likely to share the road with a dog—a large, black-and-white mutt who annually pulls his master through the fun run. The scenery is appealing too, a mixture of mountain chains, ocean vistas, and urban streets lined by three-story concrete buildings painted in earth colors and heated entirely by underground springs. The air is pure in this smokeless city, the temperature is an ideal 50 degrees, and the two-loop course is flat.

Apart from a headwind along the seacoast, the only worry left to runners is that of getting lost, a fate that befell an American named Francis Murphy. One of only seventy-eight entrants in the 1985 marathon, Murphy ran the second loop alone. Somehow he missed a directional arrow and extended his journey along a maze of back streets. Race officials eventually found him running what they estimated to be his twenty-eighth mile, and convinced him to accept a ride to the Old Centre. Oskarsson gave Murphy a finisher's medal at the awards ceremony, nicely ending the story.

The Reykjavik Marathon and Half Marathon are modest tourist successes, attracting three hundred visitors from thirteen nations. "Someday I can see two thousand people running here," says Oskarsson, a nice number, but not enough to bank on. At midlife, he left Urval Travel to become director of an association of fish processing plants. As his Viking ancestors discovered, the future lies at sea.

A Dixieland band sets an informal, charming tone, marching for runners and their families at the start by Loekjargata.

RIO DE JANEIRO, BRAZIL
RIO MARATHON

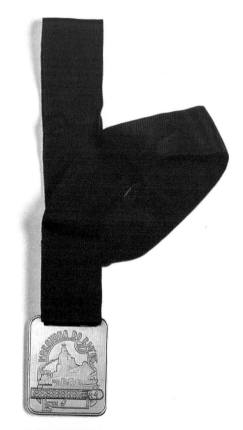

A corridor of spectators lines the road along Ipanema Beach, urging on the marathoners with shouts and applause. From beyond the seawall come other sounds, the crash of breakers and the whistle of salt spray. The high-rises shine bone-white clean in the night, as though they have just now been set on their arc of crescent shore. At beach end, rows of tiny house-lights adorn the Two Brothers Mountains like strands of electric pearls. There can be no more beautiful or improbable setting than this for a collision with the wall.

The first major, international marathon in South America, Rio was conceived in 1979 when Jose Werneck, sports columnist for *Journal Do Brasil*, accepted a Pan Am round-trip ticket to cover the Honolulu Marathon and promote the notion of flying north for a summer vacation. Werneck returned from the junket impressed by the friendly atmosphere of the race. "I wondered why we couldn't have a big-time marathon too," he says. "People thought I was crazy because Brazilians were never known for endurance sports; they would rather have fun with a ball. But I knew the potential was there. People only had to learn they could take part in such a thing."

Instead of beating the heat Hawaiian-style with a pre-dawn start,

The Rio race is disorienting: While the body adjusts to 75 degree heat, the temperature abruptly falls with the night.

Werneck decided to begin his race late in the afternoon when the beaches were still filled. "The 4 PM start was a good idea," he admits. "Right away we had tremendous crowds."

Race Director Werneck has come to call the July event "Rio's Biggest Party." Half-a-million spectators crowd a course that is dazzling right from the waterfront start. The route begins across the bay from the city in Niterói. After the Rio-Niterói Bridge, the course passes Rio's harbor, crosses the edge of the central district, continues along the coast past an airport, museum of modern art, and a war memorial, and winds through Flamengo Park between Rio's two renowned sites, Corcovado, the huge statue of Christ, and Sugar Loaf Mountain. Next comes Avenue Atlântica and the beautiful beaches of Copacabana, Ipanema, and Leblon.

"The race gets definition when the runners reach Copacabana," Werneck says. "A breeze blows in from the sea and suddenly it's night. This is where Bill Rodgers dropped out the year after he set the course record."

"When it gets dark you're not able to concentrate," says Kathy Molitor, a 2:41:00 marathoner from Houston who has run four Rio Marathons and been a TV analyst for a fifth. "You don't feel like you're in control; your body is still trying to adjust to the 70- to 80-degree heat when suddenly the temperature cools down. It's disorienting."

Molitor has noticed another phenomenon that comes with the nightfall—the macho males quietly slip away. "For 25K there are all kinds of people running with me because they don't want a woman to beat them. Then they're gone. Brazilians are emotional and excitable. The marathon is still new to them. They haven't learned to

A highlight of the marathon-long tour of Rio's beautiful waterfront is the view, at 23 kilometers, of Sugar Loaf Mountain from Flamengo Park.

Overleaf: Also visible from Flamengo, behind the runners and beyond Botafogo's beachfront, is Corcovado, a mountain from which a giant statue of Christ blesses the city.

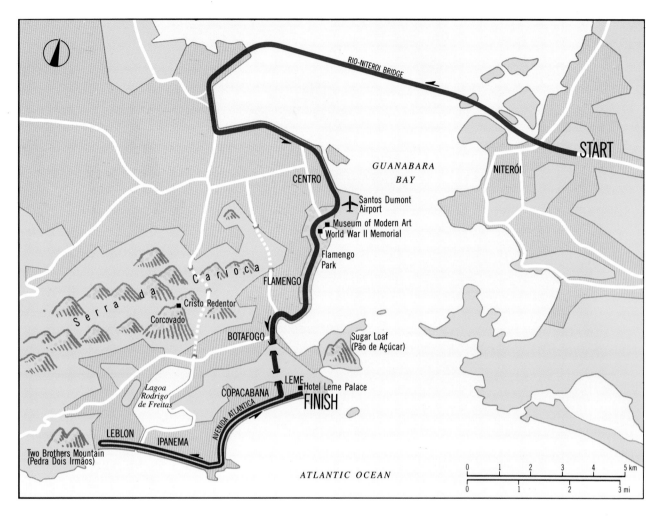

Rio Marathon

ORGANIZER *Rio Marathon*
Journal Do Brasil
500 Avenida Brasil
Rio de Janeiro 20949
Brazil
RACE DIRECTOR Jose Werneck
DATE Usually the third Saturday in July.
START 4:00 PM at Niterói.
FINISH Leme Beach.
TIME LIMIT Six-and-a-half hours.
ELIGIBILITY Open to runners of all abilities; runners must be fifteen years old by raceday.

AWARDS Awards to top finishers in all age groups, also awards to top teams and local runners. Medals to all finishers. Official certificate mailed to each finisher.
RACE RECORDS Ron Tabb, USA, 2:16:15 (1985); Patti Catalano, USA, 2:38:44 (1985).

TEMPERATURE 75°F (24°C)
CROWD 500,000
TERRAIN Flat except for a gradual, 5-kilometer climb at the start on the Rio-Niterói Bridge.
COMPETITORS 7,000 from twenty nations.
REFRESHMENTS AND SERVICES Water every 5 kilometers, sponges at 17 and 34 kilometers, sports drink at 25 and 30 kilometers; post-race jackets, cola, mineral water, sports drink, fruit, sandwiches.

ENTERTAINMENT Three bands along the way.
ADDITIONAL EVENTS Runners' mercantile expo, clinics, Friday evening pasta party, simultaneous half-marathon, slide show, awards ceremony.
UNUSUAL FEATURE The after-dark finish.

pace themselves."

Molitor describes the Rio finish as "the most dramatic I've ever seen." Suffering from dehydration, hundreds of spent runners wobble across the finish line, collapse, and are carried off to a huge medical tent, where medics scurry between the cots, connecting intravenous fluids to limp arms.

Even a segment of the audience has difficulty keeping itself in check. Each year scores of bicyclists try to pedal alongside the leader. American Greg Meyer literally fought to the finish of the first Rio Marathon in 1980, punching a biker who blocked his way. Motorcycle police have safely escorted recent leaders all the way to Leblon and back to the finish at Leme.

Behind the cops come a field of seven thousand runners, three hundred of them foreigners. There is growth potential in that last statistic, Werneck believes. "I think it's possible to attract as many as one thousand," he says. "Rio is quite a power. A Pan Am survey asked where people would most like to go in the world if they could afford to go anywhere. Rio ranked fifth. I think the reason is the landscape—our mountains, sea, and sun. Even the name 'Rio' seems to promise something wonderful."

For marathoners at least, Rio delivers.

Late on a winter's Saturday in July and early on in the event, the leaders run through Rio's golden light.

ROME, ITALY

ROME MARATHON

A street-sweeper by the Spanish Steps is distracted by a noise in the sky. He stops work, squints into the sunlight, and watches a helicopter flying low, at an odd angle. He can see that there is a television camera poking out the side. A police car and two motorcycles zoom across the narrow square, followed by a van decorated with the logo of the Ellesse sportswear company; a man sits cross-legged on its roof and babbles foreign names into the van's loudspeakers. Next arrival: Army Jeeps stacked with cliques of photographers and journalists, a station wagon hauling a digital clock, and a motorcycle carrying a portly, helmeted passenger who aims a compact TV camera at the leader, the first of two thousand runners who will cross the cobbles.

Because it is early on a Sunday—too early even for tourists—the only other pedestrians in the Piazza di Spagna are two priests, who also gape at the surreal procession, stunned. "Fellini!" someone says.

The Rome Marathon was actually dreamed up by one Franco Fava, a gaunt wisp of a man with hollow eyes and an overflowing, brown mustache, the physical antithesis of the great film director. But there are similarities as well, beginning with Fava's unflinching

Left: The 1986 leaders flee the Colosseum, ancient scene of more dangerous forms of epic competition as well as the disastrous marathon debut of 1982.

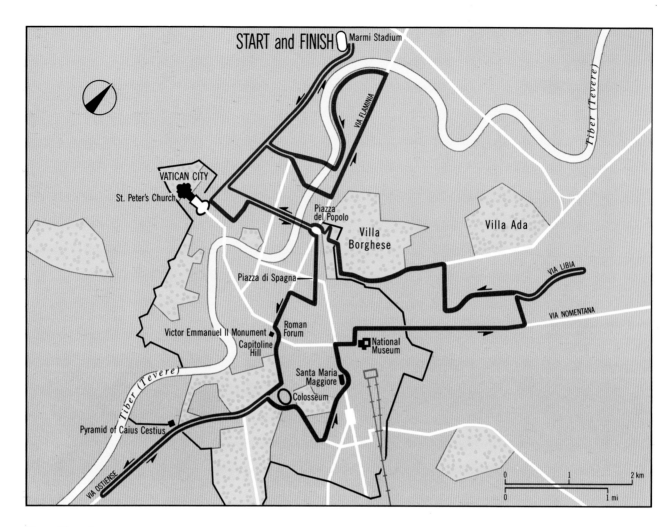

START and FINISH · Marmi Stadium

Rome Marathon

ORGANIZER *Rome Marathon*
      1325/c Via Salaria
      00138 Rome
      Italy
RACE DIRECTOR Franco Fava
DATE First day of May.
START 9:00 AM at Marmi Stadium.
FINISH Marmi Stadium.
TIME LIMIT None.
ELIGIBILITY Open to runners of all abilities; runners must be eighteen years old by raceday.

AWARDS Awards to top finishers in all age groups. Medals to all finishers.
COURSE RECORDS Michael Heilmann, East Germany, 2:11:28 (1985); Katrin Doerre, East Germany, 2:30:11 (1985).

TEMPERATURE 70°F (21°C)
CROWD 100,000
TERRAIN Mostly flat with four gradual hills: a ½-kilometer rise at the Colosseum (9 and 16 kilometers), a 1½-kilometer rise on Merulana (16½ to 18 kilometers), a 1-kilometer rise on Porta Pia (19 to 20 kilometers), and a 2-kilometer rise on Trieste and Regina Margherita (25 to 27 kilometers).
COMPETITORS 2,000 from twenty nations.
REFRESHMENTS AND SERVICES Water every 5 kilometers beginning at the 5-kilometer point, sports drink every 5 kilometers beginning at the 7½-kilometer point, sponges every 2½ kilometers beginning just beyond the 6-kilometer point; post-race sports drink, fruit, tea.

ENTERTAINMENT None.
ADDITIONAL EVENTS Simultaneous 7-kilometer fun run starting and ending in Marmi Stadium, awards ceremony.
UNUSUAL FEATURE Two thousand years of civilization en route.

confidence in his creation and, coincidentally, his habit of emerging from innumerable production crises with the product intact.

"We have our problems," says Fava, press director for the Italian Athletic Federation. "Closing the course to traffic is the biggest. The political situation often changes, shifting from left wing to right wing. It seems I'm always dealing with new people. It's difficult to put on a race like this in Rome. In New York, you have the whole town with you. Here the town doesn't participate so much. People are apathetic. We don't have volunteers; everyone must be paid or they won't help. This makes for a lot of trouble. We are missing the enthusiasm volunteers bring to a race. Even the ten jogging clubs who work the water stations expect to receive contributions. There is another problem with the clubs. Because they are rivals, they won't work together." Whenever Fava feels overwhelmed, he might think back to the marathon's debut, an epic nightmare worthy of Federico Fellini himself.

In 1982, Fava decided that Rome should have a marathon. His opinion mattered in Italian athletic circles. He was the eighth-place finisher in the 1976 Olympic Marathon in Montreal, had set national records at six distances on the track, and was a founder of *Correre* magazine as well as a TV commentator for *Domenica Sportiva*. Two thousand runners entered the 1982 Rome Marathon, which was to begin and end at the Colosseum. No problem there. The difficulty arrived with the 38,000 who showed up for a seven-kilometer fun run Fava had promoted to draw an on-the-spot crowd to the marathon's finish. Too bad the distance wasn't 8½.

"The number of fun runners was completely unexpected," Fava says. "All those people made both races unmanageable, and scared the city from letting us use the Colosseum area again." Undaunted by the best-attended flop in marathon history, Fava moved the start/

"Where's Papa?" is a question expressed by concerned faces along marathon courses in Rome and around the world.

The event competes for tourist attention with sweeping attractions like the Monument to Victor Emmanuel II, a celebration of Italian independence completed in 1911.

finish across the Tevere River to Marmi Stadium, and turned the annual fun run into a secret shared by five thousand entrants.

After weathering that stormy launch, no sea seemed unnavigable. Fava coddled traffic officials, won Ellesse's continued loyalty as the marathon's single sponsor, kept the clubs at bay, and captured the support of the Army. He managed a raceday organization that each year safely saw two thousand runners from twenty nations through the 70-degree warmth. And without room in his $150,000 budget for advertising, Fava counted on the majestic course to sell itself. "This is a run past two thousand years of civilization," Fava trumpets.

From Marmi Stadium, built by Mussolini and ringed by sixty strapping, marble jocks, the first half of the route passes St. Peter's Square, crosses the river and sightsees the Piazza del Popolo, the Piazza di Spagna, the Monument to Victor Emmanuel II, Capitoline Hill, the Roman Forum, the Colosseum (twice), the Pyramid of Caius Cestius, the Church of Santa Maria Maggiore, and the National Museum. The price a runner pays for the historic tour is the discomfort of cobblestones for one-third of the way. Rome's hills are easier to take. Only four of "the seven" are included, none excessively steep or long. Part two is mostly downhill, cobble-free, and even pastoral along Via Nomentana and the Villa Borghese.

When the World Championships take place in Rome in 1987, the marathon will be raced on Fava's course. He will share something more with Fellini then, if only for a couple of televised hours—an international following.

Just beyond the Tevere River at 6 kilometers comes the Piazza del Popolo, statuesque scene of the first sponge station.

ROTTERDAM, NETHERLANDS

CITY OF ROTTERDAM MARATHON

The City of Rotterdam Marathon is the ultimate speed trip, a race for the serious-minded runner whose attention is focused primarily on the clock. Here are ideal conditions for a personal-best time: a negative altitude (the city is six meters below sea level); a course that is almost entirely flat (ramps of a bridge are the only inclines); a crowd representing most of the population (400,000 of Rotterdam's 550,000 residents turn out); a limited field to guarantee minimal congestion and maximum service (only half of the 8,000 entry requests are accepted); and the inspiration of a world record (Carlos Lopes' 2:07:12).

Rotterdam's fast reputation was established early on. In 1983, just two years after the event was launched by three local running clubs, the race had a big-time sponsor in Nike and the two dominant marathoners of the day, Alberto Salazar and Robert de Castella. The Australian won the confrontation in 2:08:37, then the third-best time ever, outsprinting not Salazar, who finished fifth, but Lopes, a thirty-six-year-old newcomer to the distance.

Lopes had become Portugal's first Olympic medalist by winning the silver in the 10,000-meters at the 1976 Games in Montreal. Since then the five-foot-six, one-hundred-twenty-one-pound runner

Sharing the historic fifth running in Rotterdam were the 2,600 starters who followed Portugal's Carlos Lopes from the start on Coolsingel Street.

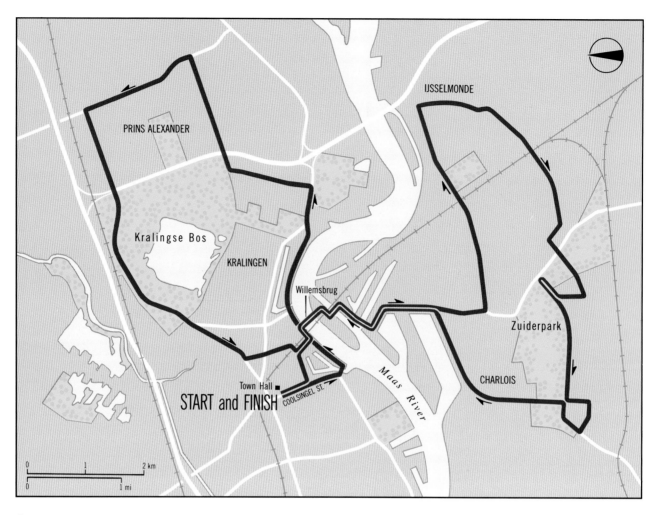

City of Rotterdam Marathon

ORGANIZER *Rotterdam Marathon*
Post Office Box 1627
Rotterdam 3000 BP
Netherlands
RACE DIRECTOR Mario Kadiks
DATE Third Saturday in April.
START 3:00 PM at the Town Hall.
FINISH Town Hall.
TIME LIMIT Five hours.
ELIGIBILITY Open to runners of all abil-
ities; runners must be eighteen years old
by raceday.

AWARDS Awards to top finishers in all age
groups, also awards to top teams and
local runners. Medals to all finishers.
Official results booklet mailed to each
finisher.
COURSE RECORDS Carlos Lopes, Portugal,
2:07:12 (1985); Ellinor Lungros, Sweden,
2:41:06 (1986).

TEMPERATURE 60°F (15°C)
CROWD 400,000
TERRAIN Completely flat except for slight
rises onto Willemsbrug Bridge.
COMPETITORS 4,000 from twenty nations.
REFRESHMENTS AND SERVICES Water, mineral water, bananas, and pineapples
every 5 kilometers, sponges midway between each water station; post-race
blankets, massages, showers.

ENTERTAINMENT None.
ADDITIONAL EVENTS Simultaneous 15-
kilometer recreation run; awards ceremony.
UNUSUAL FEATURE Ideal conditions for a
personal-best time.

had been bedeviled by injury and disappointment. Among those who urged him to move up to the marathon was his friend Jos Hermens, Nike's man in Rotterdam.

After Lopes' brilliant 2:08:39 debut, race and runner continued to be intertwined, in both good times and bad. Lopes returned to Rotterdam in 1984, hoping for a world record. But he suffered a cramp and dropped out at 17½ miles. During his triumphant visit to Los Angeles that summer, the brand-new Olympic champion told Hermens that the three-lap course was a bore. Redesigned to stroke Lopes' psyche, Rotterdam 1985 began at the Town Hall and wound around four of the city's nine districts. More than fresh scenery convinced Lopes to join 2,600 runners at the start. He reportedly received $50,000 to appear, and rumor flew of a $50,000 bonus if he broke the Steve Jones record of 2:08:05. Lopes would be further helped along by two Belgians assigned to set the early pace and shield the wind. Cooperation was everywhere, even in the cool, calm weather. All Lopes would say about a record on his lucky third try was, "We'll see."

Missing from the crowded scene at the front of the 1985 field is leader Lopes, who is nearing the 5-mile mark and already well out of reach.

2:07:11

ERATON

'n schoon eindpunt

Stad Rotterdam
Marathon

1985 ROTTERDAM 1985

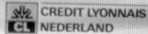

CREDIT LYONNAIS
NEDERLAND

Lopes sailed across the flat, colorful port city—rebuilt after the Second World War, the modern buildings are painted blue, orange, or yellow—reaching the halfway point in 1:03:24. His final five-kilometer split (15:20 between 35 and 40 kilometers) was only ten seconds outside record pace, minimal slippage at that late stage. The section contained eye-stopping structures—the Willemsbrug, a bridge that has become the symbol of born-again Rotterdam, and Pieter Blom's cubist houses along the Maas River.

In the final two kilometers, Lopes' legs tightened and strain peeked across his stoic expression. Arms pumping, shock of hair bouncing, he ran along Coolsingel Street through a tunnel of crowd noise. He finished before jammed one thousand-seat viewing stands with the faintest smile on his lips. A few steps across the line, he was mobbed by officials. Race Director Gerard Rooijakkers threw an arm around the winner, who did nothing more dramatic than clear his nose. When Lopes saw his wife, he nodded and accepted a kiss on the cheek.

The reaction of everyone else in the running world was considerably more spirited. Other elite runners shook their heads in wonder at a Lopes post-race comment: "With some more good runners in the race, I think I could have gone even faster—perhaps two minutes faster." Noting that in barely more than a year he also had run the second-fastest 10,000-meters on record (27:17.48) and had won two world cross-country championships along with the Olympics, history buffs proclaimed him one of the greatest distance runners of all time. Baby-boomers took comfort in Lopes' ability to accomplish all that as he neared forty. Carbo-loaders were horrified to learn he had eaten a steak the night before the race. Skeptics spread the rap—disproved by remeasurement—that the course was short.

A post-record depression settled over the event. Suddenly there was nothing left to aim for. Nike withdrew its sponsorship. Rooijakkers retired, saying, "Running a marathon is harder than running in a marathon." Most of his troubles were rooted in Rotterdam's soft, damp earth. Asphalt crumbles each spring, creating a race director's nightmare. On that memorable April Saturday, Lopes ran about 10 kilometers on roads that were under repair. One week before the race, Rooijakkers was informed that a bridge would have to be closed to traffic, his runners included. "In five years, I aged ten," he adds.

The title of race director was tossed to a twenty-six-year-old javelin thrower, Mario Kadiks, who accepts his lot with humor. "No one could deny we have a dynamic event," he says. "Even our course is in constant motion." Godspeed.

Arms pumping and legs tightening, Lopes is a tick away from lowering the world record by 53 seconds, earning a rumored $50,000 bonus, and comforting his fellow baby-boomers.

SAN FRANCISCO, CALIFORNIA

SAN FRANCISCO MARATHON

To reach the spectacular Fort Point turn-around runners endured a fifteen-to-twenty-mph headwind for 3 miles until 1986 when a drastic rerouting sacrificed scenery for comfort.

San Francisco is a city of paradoxes. Crowded onto the hilly tip of a peninsula, it rises from topography unsuited to urban growth. Summer heat arrives in autumn. The most recognizable structure, the Golden Gate Bridge, is usually hidden in fog. Alcatraz Island, the uninviting site of an abandoned prison, is a major tourist attraction. The most original modern skyscraper, the Transamerica Building, is shaped like an ancient, albeit anorexic, pyramid. This city is where it all began for a long-lived rock band called The Grateful Dead. As for the local marathon, it may be the premier 26.2-mile race in the West, but it isn't even the biggest roadshow in town.

San Francisco only goes bonkers over one running race, the Bay to Breakers. Each May 85,000 costumed crazies jog their imaginations from Fisherman's Wharf to Ocean Beach, a distance of 7.5 miles. Even front-of-the-packers catch the spirit: Joan Benoit came as a Maine lobster, and barely clawed her way to victory over a half-dozen males dressed as a centipede. Imagine having to follow that act out onto the streets.

Such is the fate of the San Francisco Marathon, a race with *only* six thousand entrants, most of whom dress only to run. When the

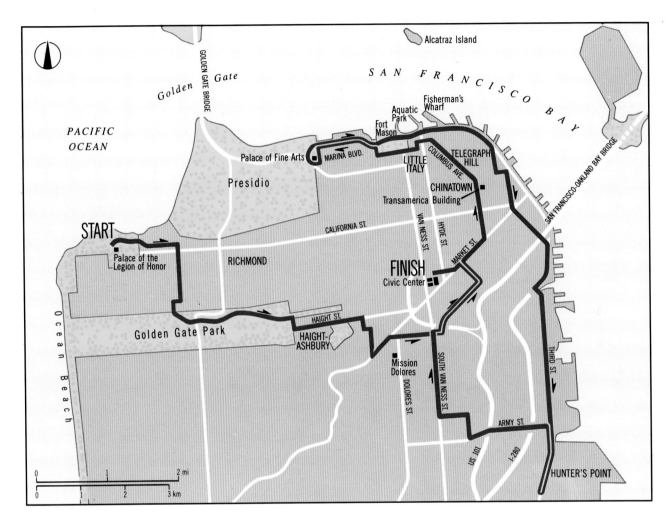

San Francisco Marathon

ORGANIZER *Pamakid Runners Club*
1233 Taraval Street
San Francisco, CA
94116-2442
USA

RACE DIRECTOR Scott Thomason
DATE Third Sunday in July.
START 8:00 AM at the Palace of the Legion of Honor.
FINISH Civic Center, UN Plaza.
TIME LIMIT None.
ELIGIBILITY Open to runners of all abilities; runners must be sixteen years old by raceday.

AWARDS Awards to top finishers in all age groups. Medals to all finishers. Official certificate and results magazine mailed to each finisher.
COURSE RECORDS Simeon Kigen, Kenya, 2:10:17 (1984); Janis Klecker, USA, 2:35:43 (1983).

TEMPERATURE 60°F (15°C)
CROWD 10,000
TERRAIN Downhill for first 8 miles, grades through mile 13 concluding with steep Fort Mason Hill, flat through mile 20, hilly through mile 22, flat to finish.
COMPETITORS 6,000 from twenty-five nations.
REFRESHMENTS AND SERVICES Water and electrolyte drink every other mile; post-race blankets, snacks, beer, mineral water, and massages.

ENTERTAINMENT Ten bands along the way.
ADDITIONAL EVENTS Runners' mercantile expo and clinics, 3-mile Saturday morning Breakfast Run and T-shirt swap for out-of-towners from Marina Green to Ft. Point and back, awards ceremony, disco party.
UNUSUAL FEATURE Digital clocks displaying time and pace at every mile.

marathon rolls around town early on a July Sunday, San Franciscans roll over and pull the sheets over their heads. "Unlike the Bay to Breakers, the marathon is too far for pure fun," says Race Director Scott Thomason. "If people in the Bay Area aren't taking part in something, they have no interest in watching it." As a result, the marathon is vacuum-packed. Apart from the echoed cheers from clumps of relatives, the runners hear only their own footsteps.

Not just an audience is missing from the course. Gone too are the city's infamous hills, a more welcome omission. Like most everything on display—the cable cars, the vertical gardens, the topless body of Carol Doda—the marathon route is an ingenious triumph over gravity. "We wanted to showcase the city as much as we could without making the course too difficult," says Thomason. "What we did was cut through the valleys between the hills."

Thomason's trail has a net elevation loss of 300 feet, a statistic accomplished by zigzagging through forty sharp curves. Around the bends are a dizzying number of historic landmarks and neighborhoods. Starting at the Palace of the Legion of Honor with a view of the Golden Gate Bridge, fog permitting, the course passes through Chinatown, Little Italy, Fisherman's Wharf, and Aquatic Park. After the mansions of Marina Boulevard, the route concludes its westward leg at the Palace of Fine Arts, a Roman ruin built for the 1915 Pan Pacific Exposition. The course then about-faces, returning along the waterfront to the financial district and continuing on to a black community called Hunter's Point. The course finishes among the stately marble buildings of the Civic Center.

The race makes up for lost crowds with superior service provided by 2,500 volunteers. San Francisco was the first marathon to produce digital clocks and pace times at every mile mark. A perfectionist, Thomason has been refining the course since 1982, the year he moved the race out of Golden Gate Park. A proposed future improvement is the elimination of Fort Mason Hill—a grueling obstacle where many races had been decided—by spending $10,000 to pave the way through an obsolete water tunnel. "A big expense for a race that is just breaking even, but worth it," he says.

Avoiding the hills means also avoiding the city's residential neighborhoods, where most San Franciscans live. Loneliness is a severe test that marathoners will have to endure. "The only way to get a crowd is to flatten the city," admits the race director. "I'm thinking of starting the race later in the day. Might help."

Thomason likes to describe San Francisco as the most tolerant of cities. Surely, he still hopes, there must be some room left in her ample heart for his marathon.

One third of the way into the race is the North Beach district and the Condor Club, where dancer Carol Doda has long hung out.

Cheered by a banner finish at the Civic Center, runners follow the red-brick road past the Opera House, where in 1945 the United Nations was founded.

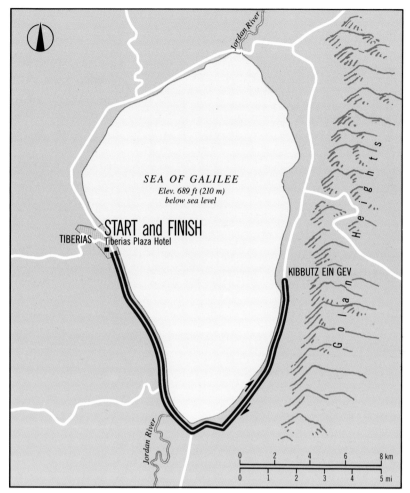

Tiberias Marathon

ORGANIZER *Tiberias Marathon*
Shartours
6 Shmuel Hanatziv Street
Netanya 42281
Israel
RACE DIRECTOR Amos Krize
DATE Midweek in early December.
START 9:00 AM at the Tiberias Plaza
Hotel.
FINISH Tiberias Plaza.
TIME LIMIT Five hours.
ELIGIBILITY Open to runners of all abilities; runners must be sixteen years old
by raceday.

AWARDS Awards to top finishers in all age
groups, also awards to top local runners.
Medals and official certificates to all finishers.
COURSE RECORDS Kevin Shaw, Zimbabwe,
2:14:02 (1978); Chantal Langlace,
France, 2:41:58 (1983).

TEMPERATURE 60°F (15°C)
CROWD 2,500
TERRAIN Flat except for a 400-meter hillock near the Jordan River and a ¼-mile
slope from/to Tiberias.
COMPETITORS 600 from fifteen nations.
REFRESHMENTS AND SERVICES Water and
sponges every 3 kilometers.

ENTERTAINMENT School bands and dancers at the start and finish.
ADDITIONAL EVENTS Raceday eve pasta
party featuring folk dancing, free entry to
the Tiberias Hot Springs, awards ceremony.
UNUSUAL FEATURE The lowest international marathon (210 meters below sea
level).

SEA OF GALILEE, ISRAEL
TIBERIAS MARATHON

A decade ago, Barry Shaw left a giftware salesman's job in Manchester, England, and went to work in the banana fields of a kibbutz on the eastern shore of the Sea of Galilee. The midlife move was only bananas in the literal sense. His wife Carol, who had been unhappy as a housewife once their children were grown, readily took root on the collective farm. Shaw had only one regret himself. He missed his recreation—training and competing with his fellow members of a Manchester running club.

Each evening, Shaw ran solo along the Biblical lake, and before very long guilt began piling up with the miles. "I was in my own dream world; following in the footsteps of Jesus, running where Peter fished," he says. "The Sermon-on-the-Mount mountain was off in the distance. Across the lake was Mary Magdalene's village. Nazareth was only 20 kilometers up the road. It was too wonderful a setting to be enjoyed by me alone."

Shaw decided to sell the idea of a marathon scheduled during the Christmas and Hanukkah season. The market was not regional, he was sure; Israel's only 42.195-kilometer race at the time was a seven-lapper around a village called Moshau Arugot that appealed to eight entrants, four of whom finished. Shaw sent letters abroad to

Excused from the classroom on marathon morning, the children of Tiberias assemble in the Plaza Hotel parking lot and play with a flourish.

American Charlotte Gilbert, secretary of the First Baptist Church in Richmond, California, was the first of the twenty women participants in 1985 to arrive back at the hotel.

110 runners, everyone he could think to invite to the inaugural Sea of Galilee International Marathon in 1977. A few of Shaw's friends flew in to justify the name, but most of the ninety-nine starters were Israelis, as it turned out. The race created a trickle of local interest in long-distance running. Shaw hoped that a flood might someday follow, and happily set off with the fresh ambition "to make my hobby my work in my new homeland."

Survival is success in Israel, and by that measure Shaw's marathon became a hit. At last count, six hundred runners raced around the southern end of the Sea of Galilee from the resort town of Tiberias, across the Jordan River to the Kibbutz Ein Gev and back. Included in the field were 250 foreigners from fourteen countries.

Unlike the battle-scarred Golan Heights looming beyond the turnaround point, and the automatic rifles carried by the soldiers who patrol the finish line, the numbers are not explosive. More grim evidence of instability is the white UN vehicles traveling upcourse to the Golan buffer zone between the Israel/Syria border.

The future of the event—renamed the Tiberias Marathon at the insistence of town fathers—is by no means secure. The start and finish is the driveway of the Tiberias Plaza, a five-star hotel that continues to provide a banquet hall, discount room rates, almost all of the $30,000 annual budget, and good faith that the marathon will someday fill it up. "If the Plaza ever decided that the race isn't worth its while, the race wouldn't continue," admits an Israeli Athletic Association official.

The hotel provides all the trappings of the big-time—race pro-

gram, pasta party, T-shirt, medal, prize ceremony, and result certifi-cate—but out on the course the service is no-frills. Aside from water and sponges along the way, sausage sandwiches are dispensed from an Army truck parked at 20 miles. Kilometers are marked by hand-painted signs propped up by rocks. Instead of a digital clock mounted on a sporty pace car, a Land Rover transports a passenger with a bullhorn who calls the time to the leader. Recently both the finish-line clock and the computer timing system broke down, prompting a lame quip from Race Chairman Amos Krize: "They are not Israeli-made."

The event is rich in homegrown spirit, if not backup equipment. No community anywhere gives more to its marathon than this an-cient Roman town; Tiberias donates its children. The midweek raceday is celebrated by two thousand kids who are bused to the Plaza parking lot from all eight schools. They cheer the start of the marathon and then fill the wait for the finish with music, dancing, games, and running races.

The youthful theme continues out on the course. Twenty groups of kibbutz students and teachers spread out along the lakeside and cheer the runners around the distinctive route. Tiberias is the lowest marathon in the world, located 210 meters below sea level. "There is a suggestion that if you go below sea level, you can absorb more oxygen with less effort," claims Shaw, still selling his race as head of the Israel Association of Veteran Athletes. "I have run two 2:35:00 marathons here, fifteen minutes faster than my best time anywhere else. There must be a scientific explanation."

Not necessarily. These are the waters where Jesus walked and performed other miracles, a setting that for two thousand years has inspired mortal men.

With 3 miles to go, the ancient town of Tiberias and modern Plaza is a tan-talizing sight across the Sea.

Overleaf: Beginning the trip around the southern shore of the Biblical lake, mar-athoners pass the bathhouse that will be open to them free-of-charge raceday afternoon.

STOCKHOLM, SWEDEN

STOCKHOLM MARATHON

S weden's first long-distance race took place in the 1520s. It covered fifty-five miles and was contested between a nobleman named Gustavus Vasa and the hitmen of Christian II of Denmark. Traveling the distance on wooden skis, Vasa avoided capture and glided off to lead a successful revolution against Danish rule. Patriotism became inexorably linked with the episode. Just as Americans associate independence with the midnight ride of Paul Revere, Swedes are moved by the midwinter trek of King Gustavus I.

Twelve thousand grateful Swedes annually emulate their founding exerciser with the Vasaloppet, an 88-kilometer cross-country ski race that began in the 1920s. Two million more—one quarter of the population—reflect their heritage by participating in sports in general. Soccer, tennis, and running have become the top three warmweather choices in the 1980s.

Proclaimed the world's best running city by *The Runner* magazine in 1986, Stockholm boasts nearly two hundred running races, three to five every weekend from April to November. Most crowded on the schedule are the Lidingoloppet 30K (21,000 starters), cross-country racing's record field; the Tjejmilen 10K for women (8,400), bigger

Above: National hero Ingemar Johansson started five of the first eight marathons, and his three finishes inspired thousands of Swedes to hit the road. Right: Midway through the second lap, the front-runners pass the gilded columns of the Royal Dramatic Theatre on Strandvägen.

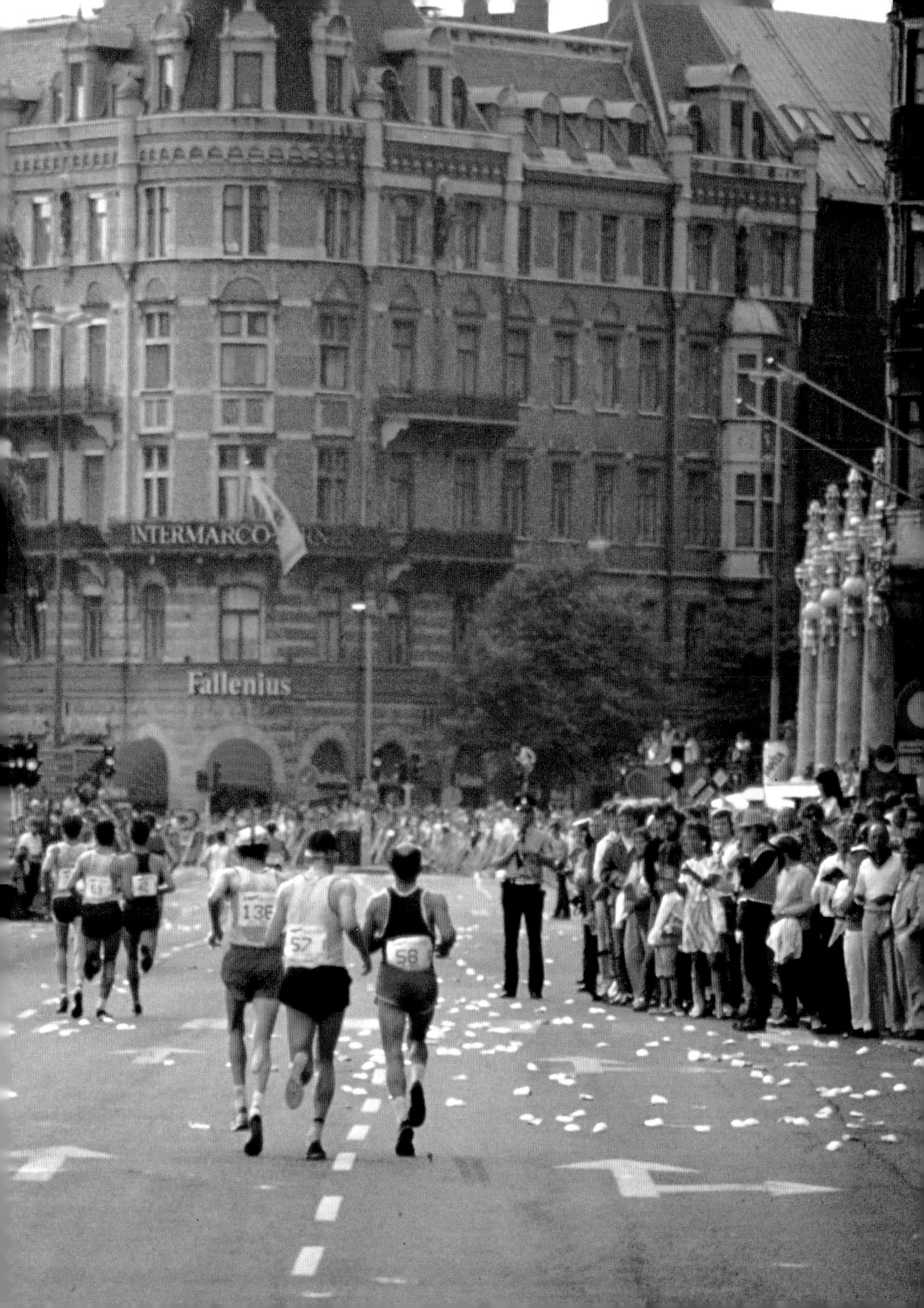
INTERMARCO
Fallenius
136
57
58

even than the pioneering L'Eggs Mini-Marathon in New York, and the Stockholm Marathon (12,000), which contains the most thrilling finish in all of marathoning.

Nearly filling Olympic Stadium, 20,000 spectators remain in their seats and in full voice to greet—especially—the back-of-the-packers. In this magical, ivy-covered place the audience delights in changing the tortoises into hares.

"I didn't think I had much left at the end," says American Lee Carlson, a vacationing lawyer who ran a 4:41:10. "It was nice to finally get to the stadium where Jim Thorpe won his gold medals way back when [in 1912]. I managed to pick up my pace a bit, but I wasn't exactly stirred by history. My legs felt pretty dead as I shuffled through a tunnel and onto the track. Then I heard something unexpected, a wall of noise. I looked up and saw thousands of cheering people. I don't know how I did it, but I turned on the afterburners and sprinted to the finish. It seemed as if the faster I went, the louder the cheers. I passed quite a few runners. Exhilaration is the only word for how I felt during those last 250 meters."

Reaching the end may not be easy, but the two laps of one of Europe's loveliest cities is hardly a bore. The setting is as diverse as the airy woods of Djurgarden, the royal park, and the narrow alleys of the Old Town. Much of the route follows the waterfront, passing buildings like the Royal Dramatic Theatre, the Royal Palace, and the City Hall where the Nobel Prizes are awarded.

Many of the 1,100 foreign marathoners prefer the human scenery. "The people lining the course were blond, beautiful, and healthy," Carlson noticed, "and looked like they could all be running the race themselves. But what especially impressed me was their energy; they were trying even harder to help us on the second lap. Everyone was shouting 'Heja!', which I think means 'Go for it!' "

"Our race shows that the top runners are not really all that important," says Race Director Anders Olsson. "It's not the elite that the 300,000 spectators are interested in. It's the masses."

A sports writer for the newspaper *Svenska Dagbladet*, Olsson discovered the concept of a mass marathon one day in 1978 while riding the Stockholm subway. "I read an article in *Sports Illustrated* about the New York City Marathon. I wondered why you have to go to New York to run a marathon. Why not have one here? The idea had a flaw, I had to admit. Despite our long tradition of fitness, Swedes believed that the marathon was just for very few, very crazy runners."

Olsson soon earned a reputation as a marketing wizard. He not only reproduced New York's roadshow, he booked superstar Bill

More than four hours after the start, a spectator patiently waits to present her husband with a gift when he arrives in Olympic Stadium.

Right: Half the race is run along the waterfront, such as here on the Söder Mälarstrand where the crowds are largest.

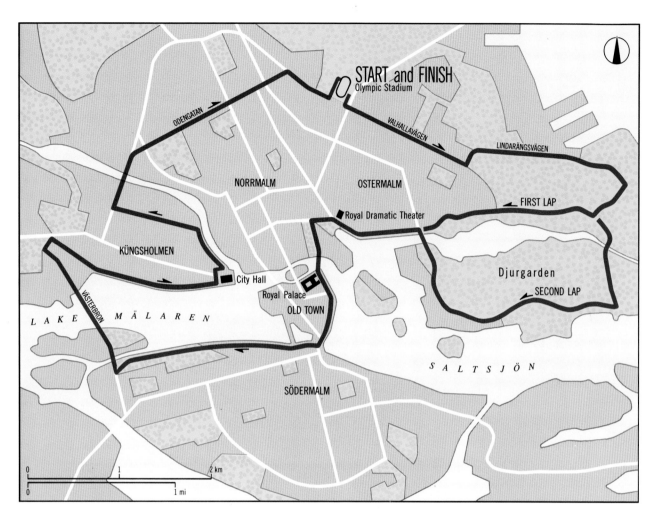

Stockholm Marathon

ORGANIZER *Stockholm Marathon*
Box 10023
S-10055 Stockholm
Sweden
RACE DIRECTOR Anders Olsson
DATE Usually the first Saturday in June.
START 3:00 PM at Olympic Stadium.
FINISH Olympic Stadium.
TIME LIMIT Five hours.
ELIGIBILITY Open to runners of all abilities; runners must be seventeen years old by the year of the race.

AWARDS Awards to top finishers in all age groups, also awards to top teams and local runners. Medals to all finishers. Official certificate and results magazine mailed to each finisher.
COURSE RECORDS Hugh Jones, Great Britain, 2:11:37 (1983); Ria van Landeghem, Belgium, 2:34:13 (1984).

TEMPERATURE 65°F (18°C)
CROWD 300,000
TERRAIN Mostly flat except for two ¾-mile climbs up Västerbron (the bridge at 12 and 33 kilometers).
COMPETITORS 12,000 from thirty-four nations.
REFRESHMENTS AND SERVICES Water and sports drink every 2 miles; post-race Danish, fruit, ice cream, yogurt, juice, massages.

ENTERTAINMENT Eight bands along the way, two more at the finish.
ADDITIONAL EVENTS Runners' mercantile expo, Friday evening pasta party, awards ceremony.
UNUSUAL FEATURE The Olympic Stadium crowd of 20,000 cheering all finishers.

Rodgers. Olsson also arranged for the timely publication of a Swedish edition of Rodgers' autobiography. He went on to produce two original hits: *Jogging* magazine and a training-tips series for the Swedish Radio Company.

Olsson annually presented live raceday appearances by rock bands in the stadium, celebrity athletes at the water stations, and Sweden's greatest sports hero—former heavyweight champion Ingemar Johansson—in the race itself. Two years in a row Olsson outdid himself, flying in boxer Floyd Patterson to compete as well. Ingo twice finished far behind his one-time rival.

Johansson was nevertheless the event's perfect pitchman. Says Olsson, "People looked at him and thought, 'If that fat old guy can run the marathon, then I could too.' " Johansson also taught the spectators that the last finishers were worth waiting for.

In 1982, with the temperature an unusual 90 degrees, runners sought relief under the showers placed every 2 miles along the course.

VIENNA, AUSTRIA

SPRING MARATHON VIENNA

The Spring Marathon Vienna is as pleasingly offbeat as the name suggests. Where else could a runner pass a world-renowned opera house, an even more famous river, a massive diplomatic complex, a space needle stuck in the midst of a botanical garden, a giant Ferris wheel, and an imperial palace? And where else could a runner be passed free beer from a brewery-staffed aid station located at 40 kilometers? And what runner could pass up an award ceremony in the palace's Great Ballroom featuring a live appearance by "the King," Elvis Presley?

Of course, it's only an impersonator who is gyrating hips on the stage and bouncing hits off the muraled ceiling and marble walls. The State Opera House is not the original either, but a restoration of the pre-Second World War structure. Other quibbles en route: The Danube is usually gray, not blue; the United Nations buildings are striped with Howard Johnsons' orange; this being only late March, the flowers in Danube Park are not in bloom; the rides in the Prater Funfair aren't open either; the beer fountain behind the finish line attracts the wrong crowd—Vienna's street people. But no one seems to mind.

The warmth of the occasion matches the beauty and variety of the

Although Austria has no tradition of long distance running, the event absorbs a surprising number of spectators and competitors.

course. Few big-city marathons are less competitive and more human than this one. When Race Director Dr. Hubert Hein is asked to recall great moments from the event, he ignores the names and times of winners and settles upon an anecdote about a non-participant, a gas station operator.

"The man was surprised to see no cars on the street, only runners," Hein begins. "The course was three laps that first year [1984], and he tried to make the best of it by putting up a table and selling cola and beer. Business was good until the third lap. By then he had become his own best customer. He was drunk." The next year, the laps were gone, the station was bypassed, and the beer became official. "I read somewhere that it's good for marathoners," Hein explains.

A second favorite story concerns the behavior of a middle-aged woman in an expensive sealskin overcoat who appeared at the runners-only, post-race refreshment area on the palace grounds. She picked over the supply until she had filled a shopping bag with bananas, cakes, and oranges. Without a word to anyone, she then walked off. "She looked a lady," says Hein. "I'm sure she saw all those people helping themselves to food, and decided she might as well join in."

Even more incongruous that first year were the volunteers assigned to welcome each finisher into the chutes. Members of a club that played, of all things, American football, they all reported in uniform including helmets and padded pants—their marathon T-shirts stretched over shoulder pads.

Another American touch was the International Breakfast Run the day before the race, an idea Hein brought home from a research trip to the New York City Marathon. He made one significant alteration. "We did away with the exercise part. Foreign entrants were invited to enjoy a big breakfast and a view of the city in the restaurant of the Danube Tower [the space needle]."

Nothing is relaxed about Hein's ambition for his event, however. He foresees a reputation almost as grand as the scenery along the Ring, the boulevard encircling the heart of the nineteenth-century Austrian Empire. "I hope Vienna will become known as the first great marathon of the year in Europe. We have 3,500 runners at the moment, too small a number for such a claim. But word will spread. By 1990, as many as 8,000 will be running here."

That such a thought is possible is a miraculous achievement in itself. When Hein, a non-practicing psychologist, dreamed up the idea of making a mass marathon in 1983, the notion seemed out of tune with reality. Austrians enjoyed racing long distances, but only

The race opens and closes in sumptuous style on the Ring, a boulevard that recalls the era when Vienna, like Paris, was a European city of imperial dreams.

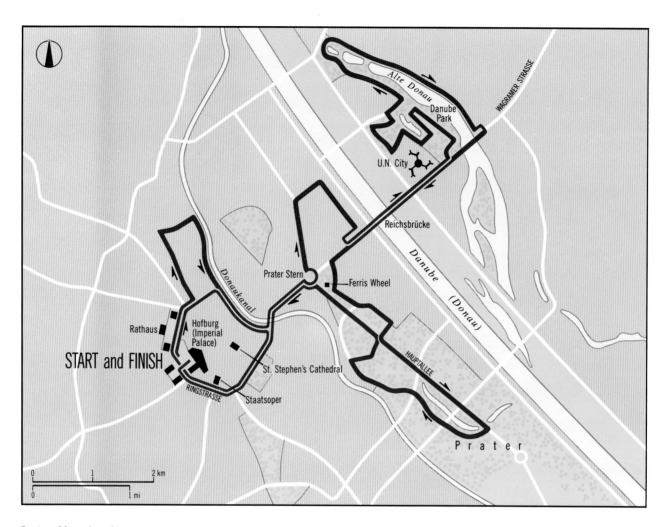

Spring Marathon Vienna

ORGANIZER *Vienna Convention Center*
Hofburg
Heldenplatz
1010 Vienna
Austria
RACE DIRECTOR Hubert Hein
DATE Usually the last Sunday in March.
START 10:00 AM at Rathausplatz (City Hall).
FINISH Heldenplatz (Place of Heroes).
TIME LIMIT Five hours.
ELIGIBILITY Open to runners of all abilities.

AWARDS Awards to top finishers in all age groups, also awards to top teams and journalists. Medals to all finishers. Official certificate and results magazine mailed to each finisher.
COURSE RECORDS Gerhard Hartmann, Austria, 2:12:22 (1986); Dunke Angelika, West Germany, 2:41:30 (1986).

TEMPERATURE 45°F (7°C)
CROWD 100,000
TERRAIN Flat except for the 2-meter Reichsbrücke Bridge.
COMPETITORS 3,500 from twenty-four nations.
REFRESHMENTS AND SERVICES Water, mineral water, tea, bananas, lemons, oranges, biscuits, and sponges every 5 kilometers and beer at 40 kilometers; post-race blankets, beer, tea, cakes, massages.

ENTERTAINMENT Two Austrian bands along the way.
ADDITIONAL EVENTS Runners' mercantile expo and clinics, Saturday International Breakfast, Saturday evening pancake party, awards ceremony, closing party.
UNUSUAL FEATURES The official beer station; the palatial awards ceremony.

down mountains on skis. Running was done mostly in pursuit of soccer balls. Of the few roadraces around, none had more than 150 participants. Only about twenty runners entered Austria's sole marathon, the national championship. "The running community was very small," says Hein, a former national track-and-field coach.

But Hein had specialized in teaching the pole vault, and was used to flings at lofty challenges. And anyway, he had a plan. He was sure that a nucleus of foreigners could be drawn to the race. The tourists would show that a marathon appealed to all sorts of normal people, even in the homeland of Freud. Interest in running would build, he hoped. He would speed the trend along by including a short fun run.

Hein had thought of everything except instant success. Of the 1,150 inaugural entrants, six hundred were Austrians. "I still have no idea where they all came from," he admits. Like the city's much-loved waltzes, the Spring Marathon Vienna struck an irresistible chord.

A grandly placed finale is the Heldenplatz, a square set before the Leopold Wing of the Imperial Palace, official residence of the president of the Republic of Austria.

T H E
FINISH

Rejoice! We conquer!
PHEIDIPPIDES, LEGENDARY GREEK MESSENGER

Resisting the wild inclination to hide from world-wide attention in the tunnel of the Los Angeles Memorial Coliseum, Joan Benoit emerged in 1984 as the first woman to finish an Olympic marathon.

THE WORLD'S BEST PERFORMANCES

The Progression of the World Record

Men

The following chart shows the best marathon times through the years, beginning with the 1908 Olympic marathon, the race that established the 26.2-mile (42.195-kilometer) distance. Four of the world's best times were set in Olympic Games by Johnny Hayes (1908), Hannes Kolehmainen (1920), and Abebe Bikila (1960, 1964). In the last fifty years, the biggest drop in time was in 1952 when Jim Peters took 4:56 off Yun Bok Suh's 1947 time. The next largest margin came in 1967 when Derek Clayton lowered Morio Shigematsu's 1965 record by 2:23. Longest lasting were Clayton's second record of 2:08:33.6 (1969–1981) and Kitei Son's 2:26:42 (1935–1947). Fusashige Suzuki's 1935 time of 2:27:49, on the other hand, stood for only three days.

In 1985, Alberto Salazar's 1981 world record was declared not officially recognized because the New York City Marathon was found to be 148 meters short on remeasurement. The following Boston Marathon winners are not included because variations of the course were short: Clarence H. DeMar (2:21:39.6 in 1911, 2:18:10 in 1922), Michael J. Ryan (2:21:18.2 in 1912), and Frank Zuna (2:18:57.6 in 1921) ran only 39.751 kilometers; Keizo Yamada (2:18:51 in 1953) ran 41.091 kilometers.

Name	Date	Place	Time
John Hayes, USA	7/24/08	London	2:55:18.4
Robert Fowler, USA	1/01/09	Yonkers, NY	2:52:45.4
James Clark, USA	2/12/09	New York	2:46:52.6
Albert Raines, USA	5/08/09	New York	2:46.04.6*
Fred Barrett, Great Britain	5/26/09	London	2:42:31
Harry Green, Great Britain	5/12/13	London	2:38:16.2
Alexis Ahlgren, Sweden	5/31/13	London	2:36:06.6
Hannes Kolehmainen, Finland	8/22/20	Antwerp, Belgium	2:32:35.8
Al Michelsen, USA	10/12/25	Port Chester, NY	2:29:01.8
Fusashige Suzuki, Japan	3/31/35	Tokyo	2:27:49
Yasuo Ikenaka, Japan	4/03/35	Tokyo	2:26:44
Kitei Son (Kee-Chung Sohn), Japan	11/03/35	Tokyo	2:26:42
Yun Bok Suh, Korea	4/19/47	Boston	2:25:39
Jim Peters, Great Britain	6/14/52	Chiswick, England	2:20:42.2
Jim Peters, Great Britain	6/13/53	Chiswick, England	2:18:40.2
Jim Peters, Great Britain	10/04/53	Turku, Finland	2:18:34.8
Jim Peters, Great Britain	6/26/54	Chiswick, England	2:17:39.4
Sergey Popov, USSR	8/24/58	Stockholm	2:15:17
Abebe Bikila, Ethiopia	9/10/60	Rome	2:15:16.2
Toru Terasawa, Japan	2/17/63	Beppu, Japan	2:15:15.8
Buddy Edelen, USA	6/15/63	Chiswick, England	2:14:28
Basil Heatley, Great Britain	6/13/64	Chiswick, England	2:13:55
Abebe Bikila, Ethiopia	10/21/64	Tokyo	2:12:11.2
Morio Shigematsu, Japan	6/12/65	Chiswick, England	2:12:00
Derek Clayton, Australia	12/03/67	Fukuoka, Japan	2:09:36.4
Derek Clayton, Australia	5/30/69	Antwerp, Belgium	2:08:33.6
Alberto Salazar, USA	10/25/81	New York	2:08:12.7*
Steve Jones, Great Britain	10/21/84	Chicago	2:08:05
Carlos Lopes, Portugal	4/20/85	Rotterdam	2:07:12

Not officially recognized.

On Patriot's Day, 1983, Joan Benoit began her two-year reign of the marathon world after a glorious run at Boston.

Women

The women's marathon record has gone down rapidly since 1964, dropping a full hour, six minutes, and thirty-nine seconds in just over twenty years. Grete Waitz did most of the recent record setting. In breaking the world mark four times in four-and-a-half years, she lowered it nine minutes and nineteen seconds. Allison Roe, like Alberto Salazar, had her 1981 world record in the New York City Marathon invalidated in 1985.

Name	Date	Place	Time
Violet Piercy, Great Britain	10/03/26	London	3:40:22
Dale Greig, Great Britain	5/23/64	Ryde, England	3:27:45
Mildred Sampson, New Zealand	7/21/64	Auckland	3:19:33
Maureen Wilton, Canada	5/06/67	Toronto	3:15:22
Anni Pede-Erdkamp, W. Germany	9/16/67	Waldniel, W. Germany	3:07:26
Caroline Walker, USA	2/28/70	Seaside, Oregon	3:02:53
Beth Bonner, USA	5/09/71	Philadelphia	3:01:42
Adrienne Beames, Australia	8/31/71	Werribee, Australia	2:46:30
Chantal Langlace, France	10/27/74	Neuf Brisach, France	2:46:24
Jackie Hansen, USA	12/01/74	Culver City, California	2:43:54.5
Liane Winter, W. Germany	4/21/75	Boston	2:42:24
Christa Vahlensieck, W. Germany	5/03/75	Dulmen, W. Germany	2:40:15.8
Jackie Hansen, USA	10/12/75	Eugene, Oregon	2:38:19
Chantal Langlace, France	5/01/77	Oyarzun, Spain	2:35:15.4
Christa Vahlensieck, W. Germany	9/10/77	West Berlin, W. Germany	2:34:47.5
Grete Waitz, Norway	10/22/78	New York	2:32:29.8
Grete Waitz, Norway	10/21/79	New York	2:27:32.6
Grete Waitz, Norway	10/26/80	New York	2:25:41
Allison Roe, New Zealand	10/25/81	New York	2:25:28.8*
Grete Waitz, Norway	4/17/83	London	2:25:28.7
Joan Benoit, USA	4/18/83	Boston	2:22:43
Ingrid Kristiansen, Norway	4/21/85	London	2:21:06

Not officially recognized.

The Twenty-Five Fastest Times

Men

Robert de Castella holds four of the twenty-five fastest times, Steve Jones holds three, while Carlos Lopes, Robleh Djama, Juma Ikangaa, Takeyuki Nakayama, Alberto Salazar, and Toshihiko Seko have two apiece. Four times on the list were run at the 1986 Tokyo Marathon. Three times were run at the World Cup in Hiroshima in 1985, and three more were achieved at the 1985 America's Marathon/Chicago. Seven of the twenty-five fastest times were run in 1986, ten in 1985, one in 1984, six in 1983, and all but one since 1980. The exception—Derek Clayton's 2:08:34 in 1969—is remarkable for its ranking so high on the all-time list after so many years.

Name	Date	Place	Time
1. Carlos Lopes, Portugal	4/20/85	Rotterdam	2:07:12
2. Steve Jones, Great Britain	10/20/85	Chicago	2:07:13
3. Taisuke Kodama, Japan	10/19/86	Beijing	2:07:35
4. Robert de Castella, Australia	4/21/86	Boston	2:07:51
5. Kunimitsu Itoh, Japan	10/19/86	Beijing	2:07:57
6. Zithulele Sinqe, South Africa	5/03/86	Port Elizabeth, SA	2:08:04
7. Steve Jones, Great Britain	10/21/84	Chicago	2:08:05*
8. Robleh Djama, Djibouti	10/20/85	Chicago	2:08:08
9. Ahmed Saleh, Djibouti	4/14/85	Hiroshima	2:08:09
10. Juma Ikangaa, Tanzania	2/09/86	Tokyo	2:08:10
11. Alberto Salazar, USA	10/25/81	New York	2:08:13**
12. Takeyuki Nakayama, Japan	4/14/85	Hiroshima	2:08:15
Willie Mtolo, South Africa	5/03/86	Port Elizabeth, SA	2:08:15
13. Steve Jones, Great Britain	4/21/85	London	2:08:16
14. Robert de Castella, Australia	12/06/81	Fukuoka	2:08:18
15. Takeyuki Nakayama, Japan	10/05/86	Seoul	2:08:21
16. Robleh Djama, Djibouti	4/14/85	Hiroshima	2:08:26
17. Toshihiko Seko, Japan	10/26/86	Chicago	2:08:27
18. Belayenh Densimo, Ethiopia	2/09/86	Tokyo	2:08:29
19. Charlie Spedding, Great Britain	4/21/85	London	2:08:33
20. Derek Clayton, Australia	5/30/69	Antwerp	2:08:34*
21. Robert de Castella, Australia	4/09/83	Rotterdam	2:08:37
22. Toshihiko Seko, Japan	2/13/83	Tokyo	2:08:38
23. Carlos Lopes, Portugal	4/09/83	Rotterdam	2:08:39
Abebe Mekonen, Ethiopia	2/09/86	Tokyo	2:08:39
Juma Ikangaa, Tanzania	10/19/86	Beijing	2:08:39
24. Takeyuki Nakayama, Japan	2/09/86	Tokyo	2:08:43
25. Robert de Castella, Australia	10/20/85	Chicago	2:08:48

*Former world record.   **Former world record not officially recognized.*

Women

Twenty of the twenty-five fastest times were set by only four women, with Grete Waitz holding seven, Ingrid Kristiansen six, Joan Benoit Samuelson four, and Rosa Mota three. Four of the twenty-five were set in the inaugural Olympic marathon for women at the 1984 Games in Los Angeles, and three of the top five were set in the 1985 America's Marathon/Chicago. Five on the list were run in 1986, four in 1985, seven in 1984, and only one before 1980.

Name	Date	Place	Time
1. Ingrid Kristiansen, Norway	4/21/85	London	2:21:06
2. Joan Benoit Samuelson, USA	10/20/85	Chicago	2:21:21
3. Joan Benoit, USA	4/18/83	Boston	2:22:43*
4. Ingrid Kristiansen, Norway	10/20/85	Chicago	2:23:05
5. Rosa Mota, Portugal	10/20/85	Chicago	2:23:29
6. Ingrid Kristiansen, Norway	5/13/84	London	2:24:26
7. Joan Benoit, USA	8/05/84	Los Angeles	2:24:52
8. Grete Waitz, Norway	4/20/86	London	2:24:54
9. Ingrid Kristiansen, Norway	4/21/86	Boston	2:24:55
10. Grete Waitz, Norway	4/17/83	London	2:25:29*
Allison Roe, New Zealand	10/25/81	New York	2:25:29**
11. Grete Waitz, Norway	10/26/80	New York	2:25:41*
12. Rosa Mota, Portugal	10/21/84	Chicago	2:26:01
13. Lisa Martin, Australia	8/01/86	Edinburgh	2:26:07
14. Joan Benoit, USA	9/12/82	Eugene	2:26:11
15. Grete Waitz, Norway	8/05/84	Los Angeles	2:26:18
16. Julie Brown, USA	6/05/83	Los Angeles	2:26:26
17. Allison Roe, New Zealand	4/20/81	Boston	2:26:46
18. Katrin Dorre, East Germany	7/21/84	East Berlin	2:26:52
19. Rosa Mota, Portugal	8/05/84	Los Angeles	2:26:57
20. Grete Waitz, Norway	10/23/83	New York	2:27:00
21. Ingrid Kristiansen, Norway	10/26/86	Chicago	2:27:08
22. Grete Waitz, Norway	10/24/82	New York	2:27:14
23. Grete Waitz, Norway	10/21/79	New York	2:27:33*
24. Ingrid Kristiansen, Norway	8/05/84	Los Angeles	2:27:34
25. Carla Beurskens, Netherlands	4/21/86	Boston	2:27:35

*Former world record.   **Former world record not officially recognized.

Ingrid Kristiansen had a world-record reason to be bubbly at the 1985 London Marathon awards ceremony.

Men

Carlos Lopes, *Rotterdam 1985*

Distance	Cumulative	5K Split
5K	14:58	14:58
10K	30:02	15:04
15K	45:29	15:27
20K	1:00:10	14:41
Half	1:03:24	
25K	1:14:57	14:47
30K	1:30:02	15:05
35K	1:45:14	15:12
40K	2:00:34	15:20
Full	2:07:12	

Overall pace per mile: 4:51

Women

Ingrid Kristiansen, *London 1985*

Distance	Cumulative	5K Split
5K	16:25	16:25
10K	32:52	16:27
15K	49:50	16:58
20K	1:06:30	16:40
Half	1:10:09	
25K	1:22:55	16:25
30K	1:39:18	16:23
35K	1:56:12	16:54
40K	2:13:18	17:06
Full	2:21:06	

Overall pace per mile: 5:23

THE CHAMPIONS

Olympic Games

1896 Athens, Greece

1. **Spiridon Louis,** *Greece* — 2:58:50
2. **Charilaos Vasilakos,** *Greece* — 3:06:03
3. **Gyula Kellner,** *Hungary* — 3:06:35

The first marathon in modern history was run, at the first modern Olympic Games, to commemorate the legendary feat of Pheidippides, the Greek courier who ran about twenty-four miles from the Plains of Marathon to Athens. For the host country, it was a matter of pride that a Greek should win this first marathon. When Spiridon Louis, a twenty-four-year-old Greek shepherd and mail carrier, who had built up his stamina by running alongside his mule while delivering letters and barrels of water, came in first, he became a national hero.

1900 Paris, France

1. **Michel Théatro,** *France* — 2:59:45
2. **Emile Champion,** *France* — 3:04:17
3. **Ernst Fast,** *Sweden* — 3:37:14

The second Olympic marathon was poorly organized, haphazardly routed, and it took twelve years for the result to be declared official. The 25-mile, 28-yard course looped Paris' Racing Club four times and meandered through the city's narrow back streets. When Michel Théatro, a twenty-three-year-old baker's delivery man, was the surprise winner, it was suggested by many that he relied heavily on his intimate knowledge of potential shortcuts.

The result was especially suspicious to Arthur Newton, an outstanding American distance runner, who thought he had taken the lead at the halfway mark and was shocked to find when he finished that he was fifth, over an hour behind Théatro. Only eight runners out of the nineteen who started in the 102-degree July heat finished the race.

1904 St. Louis, Missouri

1. **Thomas Hicks,** *USA* — 3:28:53
2. **Albert Corey,** *USA* — 3:34:52
3. **Arthur Newton,** *USA* — 3:47:33

The 1904 marathon—the same distance as the 1896 marathon, about 40 kilometers—was one of the most bizarre. Among the entrants was a five-foot-tall mailman from Cuba who ran in long trousers cut off at the knees and a long-sleeved shirt, a professional strike breaker, and two Zulu tribesmen from the World's Fair. Only fourteen of the thirty-two starters finished the grueling course that wandered over seven hills and dusty roads in 90-degree heat in late August.

Fred Lorz of New York City crossed the finish line first, looking amazingly fresh. He was about to be awarded the gold medal when it was discovered that he had hitched a ride for 11 miles of the race. Lorz claimed he finished the race as a joke but no one thought he was funny, least of all the real winner, Thomas Hicks. An English-born brass worker, he staggered in fifteen minutes after Lorz to lead an American sweep of the first three places. Buoyed by strychnine tablets, raw eggs, and brandy during the race, Hicks barely made it to the finish line, where he collapsed unconscious.

1906 Athens, Greece

1. **William Sherring,** *Canada* — 2:51:23.6
2. **John Svanberg,** *Sweden* — 2:58:20.8
3. **William Frank,** *USA* — 3:00:46.8

In a marathon (26 miles, 18 yards) run without incident, Bill Sherring, a slender railroad brakeman from Hamilton, Ontario, shared the lead with Bill Frank of the US after 15 miles. They then ran together for three miles until Sherring yelled, "Goodbye Billy," and built up a large lead he never lost. Prince George of Greece ran with him on the final lap in the stadium, just as he did with Spiridon Louis ten years earlier.

1908 London, England

1. **John Hayes,** *USA*   2:55:18.4
2. **Charles Hefferon,** *South Africa*   2:56:06.0
3. **Joseph Forshaw,** *USA*   2:57:10.4

The standard marathon distance of 26 miles, 385 yards (42.195 kilometers), was first run in the 1908 Olympics. Initially, the race was to be 26 miles from Windsor to the royal box in London's White City Stadium. The start was moved back to include Windsor Castle at the request of Queen Alexandra, who wanted her children to be able to view the start. This race also produced one of the most dramatic moments in Olympic history with the near-win of Dorando Pietri, the candy maker from Italy. An American protest upheld Hayes' victory because a staggering Pietri was helped across the finish line by British officials.

Mindful of this great race, the International Amateur Athletic Federation decreed at a conference in 1921 that the length of London's Olympic course would be the marathon's official length.

Filled with fatherly pride, Kevin Hodgman hugs thirteen-year-old Bryan after the latter's 2:58:59 finish of Auckland's 1982 Winstone Marathon.

1912 Stockholm, Sweden

1. **Kenneth McArthur,** *South Africa*   2:36:54.8
2. **Christian Gitsham,** *South Africa*   2:37:52.0
3. **Gaston Strobino,** *USA*   2:38:42.4

After 20 miles on a hot July day in which half of the sixty-eight starters dropped out, Christian Gitsham and his teammate Kenneth McArthur were all alone in the lead. When Gitsham stopped for a drink of water two miles from the Olympic Stadium, McArthur, a thirty-year-old policeman who had emigrated from Ireland, kept running and finished the twenty-four-mile, 1,723-yard course almost a minute ahead of Gitsham.

1920 Antwerp, Belgium

1. **Hannes Kolehmainen,** *Finland*   2:32:35.8
2. **Juri Lossmann,** *Estonia*   2:32:48.6
3. **Valerio Arri,** *Italy*   2:36:32.8

The longest Olympic marathon ever—26 miles, 991 yards—produced the closest finish in Olympic marathon history. Hannes Kolehmainen, the gold medalist in the 5,000-meter run, the 10,000-meter run, and the 8,000-meter cross-country eight years earlier in Stockholm, took the lead from Christian Gitsham (the marathon silver medalist in 1912) at the 30-kilometer mark and was never headed. Juri Lossmann closed fast to finish only 70 yards and 12.8 seconds behind. When Valerio Arri came in third, almost four minutes later, he did three cartwheels just beyond the finish line.

1924 Paris, France

1. **Albin Stenroos,** *Finland*   2:41:22.6
2. **Romeo Bertini,** *Italy*   2:47:19.6
3. **Clarence DeMar,** *USA*   2:48:14.0

The marathon distance finally settled at 26 miles, 385 yards in 1924, and all subsequent marathons were run at that distance. Age prevailed in Paris as Albin Stenroos, a thirty-five-year-old woodworker, won by almost six minutes over Romeo Bertini, age thirty-one, and Clarence DeMar, thirty-six. Stenroos, who had finished third in the 10,000-meters in 1912 and had not run a marathon in fifteen years before 1924, took over the lead after 12 miles and gradually built up an insurmountable margin of victory.

1928 Amsterdam, Netherlands

1. **Boughera El Quafi,** *France*   2:32:57.0
2. **Manuel Plaza,** *Chile*   2:33:23.0
3. **Martti Marttelin,** *Finland*   2:35:02.0

America's Joie Ray held the lead at the halfway point but was soon overtaken by Japan's Kanematsu Yamada. In sight of the Olympic Stadium, Yamada faded to finish fourth and

Boughera El Quafi and Manuel Plaza, the seventh- and sixth-place finishers in 1924, passed him. Running strongly, El Quafi, an Algerian-born auto mechanic and a former member of the French Foreign Legion, edged Plaza by twenty-six seconds as the pre-race favorite, Martti Marttelin, came in third.

1932 Los Angeles, California

1. **Juan Carlos Zabala**, *Argentina*   2:31:36
2. **Samuel Ferris**, *Great Britain*   2:31:55
3. **Armas Toivonen**, *Finland*   2:32:12

In a spectacular finish, the first four runners were all on the track at the same time and came in within one minute and five seconds of each other. Juan Carlos Zabala, a twenty-year-old Argentinian, finished first, nineteen seconds ahead of Sam Ferris, who beat Armas Toivonen by seventeen seconds. Toivonen came in twenty-nine seconds ahead of the fourth-place finisher, Duncan McLeod Wright of Great Britain. Zabala collapsed after breaking the tape, while Ferris looked barely winded.

1936 Berlin, Germany

1. **Kitei Son**, *Japan*   2:29:19.2
2. **Ernest Harper**, *Great Britain*   2:31:23.2
3. **Shoryu Nan**, *Japan*   2:31:42.0

Defending champion Juan Carlos Zabala, who trained in Berlin for six months before the race, took the lead early and held it for the first 17 miles before collapsing twice and finally dropping out. Forced to run for Japan by the occupying Japanese, Korea's Kitei Son (born Kee-Chung Sohn) took over the lead and went on to win easily by more than two minutes over thirty-four-year-old Ernest Harper, who staggered in with a badly blistered foot ahead of another Korean, Shoryu Nan.

1948 London, England

1. **Delfo Cabrera**, *Argentina*   2:34:51.6
2. **Thomas Richards**, *Great Britain*   2:35:07.6
3. **Etienne Gailly**, *Belgium*   2:35:33.6

Etienne Gailly, a twenty-five-year-old Belgian paratrooper running his first marathon, entered Wembley Stadium first. He had held an early lead until 18 miles, and regained the lead within sight of the Stadium. Gailly was 50 yards ahead of Delfo Cabrera, a twenty-nine-year-old fireman, also running his first marathon, and 100 yards ahead of Tom Richards, a thirty-six-year-old Welsh nurse.

But Gailly suddenly slowed to a walk on the final lap, reminding many of Dorando Pietri forty years earlier. Cabrera passed him to finish first. Richards did the same, coming in second. Gailly wobbled to the finish line next, forty-two seconds behind Cabrera.

1952 Helsinki, Finland

1. **Emil Zatopek**, *Czechoslovakia*   2:23:03.2
2. **Reinaldo Gorno**, *Argentina*   2:25:35.0
3. **Gustav Jansson**, *Sweden*   2:26:07.0

In an extraordinary feat of long-distance running, Emil Zatopek, a twenty-nine-year old Czech soldier, won the 5,000-meter and 10,000-meter runs and then took the marathon, all within eight days of each other. What's more, he set Olympic records in all three events, smashing the marathon mark by over six minutes while finishing two-and-a-half minutes and some 750 yards ahead of the second-place runner.

Never having run a marathon before, Zatopek, who always looked to be in extreme agony when he ran, followed the pace of Jim Peters of Great Britain, who had run the world's fastest marathon six weeks earlier. When he found the pace too slow for him about halfway through the race, Zatopek took off and was never headed. He was signing autographs when Reinaldo Gorno, the surprise silver medalist, entered the stadium. Defending champion Delfo Cabrera, though he cut more than eight minutes from the time that won him his victory four years earlier, finished only sixth.

1956 Melbourne, Australia

1. **Alain Mimoun**, *France*   2:25:00
2. **Franjo Mihalic**, *Yugoslavia*   2:26:32
3. **Veikko Karvonen**, *Finland*   2:27:47

After finishing second to Emil Zatopek three times in the Olympics (10,000-meters in 1948, 5,000- and 10,000-meters in 1952), Alain Mimoun, a thirty-five-year-old Algerian, finally beat him to the tape. Mimoun, running his first marathon, took the lead shortly before the halfway mark and easily held it the rest of the way.

When Zatopek, who had had a hernia operation six weeks earlier, came in four-and-a-half minutes later in sixth place, he saluted Mimoun and the two friendly rivals embraced. "For me," said Mimoun, "that was better than the medal."

1960 Rome, Italy

1. **Abebe Bikila**, *Ethiopia*   2:15:16.2
2. **Rhadi Ben Abdesselem**, *Morocco*   2:15:41.6
3. **Barry Magee**, *New Zealand*   2:17:18.2

This was the first Olympic marathon to be run at night, to start and end outside an Olympic stadium, to be won by a black African, and to be run under 2:20:00. The spectacular course skirted the historic ruins of Rome and finished in moonlight under the Arch of Constantine, near the Colosseum.

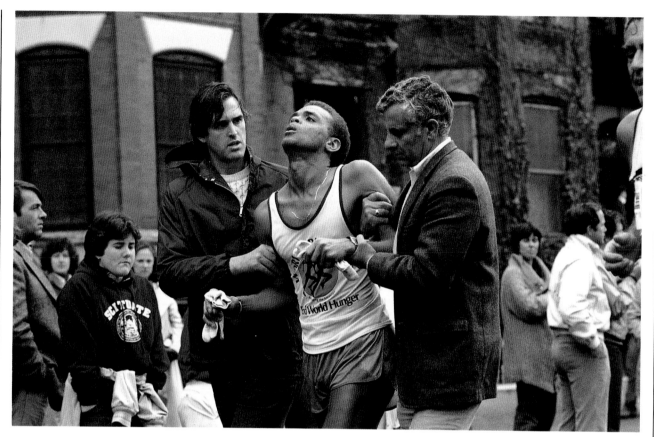

On the way to finish is the Wall, the well publicized fatigue zone between 18 and 23 miles, which sometimes, as with this Boston marathoner, is immovable.

Running barefoot all the way, Abebe Bikila, a twenty-eight-year-old private in Emperor Haile Selassie's Household Guard, pulled away from Rhadi Ben Abdesselem, who had been running with him side by side for most of the race, less than a mile from the finish line. Bikila finished some 200 yards ahead in a world record time that cut seven minutes and forty-seven seconds off Emil Zatopek's old Olympic mark. "We are a poor people and we run everywhere," he said. "Twenty-six miles is nothing to me. I could have kept going for a long time."

1964 Tokyo, Japan

1. **Abebe Bikila**, *Ethiopia*   2:12:11.2
2. **Basil Heatley**, *Great Britain*   2:16:19.2
3. **Kokichi Tsuburaya**, *Japan*   2:16:22.8

Despite having had his appendix removed five weeks earlier, Abebe Bikila, running with shoes and socks this time, shattered his 1960 Olympic record and set a new world best in finishing over four minutes ahead of runner-up Basil Heatley. Bikila was so fresh after winning his second Olympic marathon in a row, he did strenuous stretching exercises in the infield while waiting for Heatley to finish. "I could have kept up my pace for another 10 kilometers," said Bikila.

1968 Mexico City, Mexico

1. **Mamo Walde**, *Ethiopia*   2:20:26.4
2. **Kenji Kimihara**, *Japan*   2:23:31.0
3. **Michael Ryan**, *New Zealand*   2:23:45.0

Mamo Walde, thirty-six, had first competed in the Olympics in 1956, finishing last in his heats of the 800- and the 1,500-meter runs. He did not finish the 1964 marathon and placed fourth in the 10,000-meters. A week before the 1968 marathon, Walde gained the silver medal in the 10,000-meters as he came in only four yards behind Naftali Temu of Kenya.

The two Africans ran side by side in the marathon, Walde taking the lead at about the halfway mark. Temu faded to nineteenth place, while Walde went on to win easily by over three minutes. Abebe Bikila, his famous teammate trying for his third marathon win in a row, was forced to drop out with a leg injury after 10 miles.

1972 Munich, West Germany

1. **Frank Shorter**, *USA*   2:12:19.8
2. **Karel Lismont**, *Belgium*   2:14:31.8
3. **Mamo Walde**, *Ethiopia*   2:15:08.4

Japan's Toshihiko Seko is carried off the track after his 1979 Fukuoka win, the second of four.

Frank Shorter, a twenty-four-year-old Yale graduate studying law at the University of Florida, gave the US its first marathon gold medal in sixty-four years when he took the lead at nine miles and coasted to an easy victory over previously undefeated Karel Lismont. Defending champion Mamo Walde ran his fastest marathon ever at age forty as he came in third, followed by another American, Kenny Moore, a half-minute behind him.

1976 Montreal, Canada

1. **Waldemar Cierpinski**, *East Germany*   2:09:55.0
2. **Frank Shorter**, *USA*   2:10:45.8
3. **Karel Lismont**, *Belgium*   2:11:12.6

Led by Waldemar Cierpinski, a twenty-five-year-old East German sports student, the first four finishers broke Abebe Bikila's 1964 Olympic marathon record. Cierpinski, who lowered the Olympic mark by nearly two-and-a-half minutes, ran through the rain with defending champion Frank Shorter for a few miles. Then, after 21 miles, he took the lead and steadily drew away from Shorter.

Confused at the finish, Cierpinski ran an extra lap and was shocked to find Shorter waiting to congratulate him as he crossed the finish line the second time. Lasse Viren, who had won the 5,000- and 10,000-meters for the second Olympics in a row, tried the marathon for the first time and came in fifth in 2:13:10.8, only twenty-four hours after claiming his 5,000-meter victory. Missing from the Olympics were all of black Africa's outstanding distance runners, who were boycotting the Games after the International Olympic Committee refused to take action against New Zealand for participating in a rugby competition with South Africa.

1980 Moscow, USSR

1. **Waldemar Cierpinski**, *East Germany*   2:11:03
2. **Gerard Nijboer**, *Holland*   2:11:20
3. **Setymkul Dzhumanazarov**, *USSR*   2:11:35

In an extremely tight finish, the first five runners were on the track as Waldemar Cierpinski became only the second man ever to win successive Olympic marathons; only one minute and eleven seconds separated the five. A boycott by such strong track nations as the US, Japan, West Germany, and Canada, who were protesting the Soviet invasion of Afghanistan, again marred the Games.

1984 Los Angeles, California
Men

1. **Carlos Lopes**, *Portugal*   2:09:21
2. **John Treacy**, *Ireland*   2:09:56
3. **Charlie Spedding**, *Great Britain*   2:09:58

Carlos Lopes, a thirty-seven-year-old loan officer for a Lisbon bank who had completed only one marathon before the Olympics, broke Waldemar Cierpinski's eight-year-old Olympic mark by thirty-four seconds with an easy victory. As the favorites dropped back, Lopes darted ahead of the pack with about five miles to go and steadily pulled away. John Treacy, twenty-seven, running his first marathon, entered the stadium just ahead of thirty-two-year-old Charlie Spedding, and outsprinted him down the backstretch to finish second, only one second behind Cierpinski's old record. Pre-race favorite Robert de Castella of Australia came in fifth at 2:11:09. In retaliation for the 1980 Western boycott of the Moscow Games, the USSR, East Germany, and the other Eastern Bloc nations—with the exception of Rumania—staged their own boycott of the 1984 Games.

Women

1. **Joan Benoit**, *USA*   2:24:52
2. **Grete Waitz**, *Norway*   2:26:18
3. **Rosa Mota**, *Portugal*   2:26:57

In the first Olympic marathon for women, twenty-seven-year-old Joan Benoit, a five-foot-three-inch Bowdoin College graduate and the world-record holder, took the lead at the three-mile mark and breezed to an astonishingly easy win over Grete Waitz, who had never lost a marathon that she finished. "I was extremely comfortable the entire way," said Benoit. "I just sort of followed the yellow brick road." Wearing a white painter's cap, Benoit steadily ran away from the field the last 23 miles and turned in a time that would have won thirteen of the previous twenty men's Olympic marathons.

World Championships

1983 Helsinki, Finland
Men

1. **Robert de Castella**, *Australia*   2:10:03
2. **Kebede Balcha**, *Ethiopia*   2:10:27
3. **Waldemar Cierpinski**, *E. Germany*   2:10:37

Women

1. **Grete Waitz**, *Norway*   2:28:09
2. **Marianne Dickerson**, *USA*   2:31:09
3. **Raisa Smekhnova**, *USSR*   2:31:13

Robert de Castella became a legend Down Under after his dramatic battle with Kebede Balcha of Ethiopia, and double Olympic Champion Waldemar Cierpinski nipped Kjell-Erik Stahl of Sweden to win the bronze medal in the inaugural World Championships at Helsinki, Finland. In the women's competition, Grete Waitz easily won by three minutes. Marianne Dickerson, running only her third marathon, caught Raisa Smekhnova on the final bend to take second place. The next World Championships will be held in Rome in 1987.

World Cup

1985 Hiroshima, Japan
Men

1. **Ahmed Saleh**, *Djibouti*   2:08:09
2. **Takeyuki Nakayama**, *Japan*   2:08:15
3. **Robleh Djama**, *Djibouti*   2:08:26

Women

1. **Katrin Doerre**, *East Germany*   2:33:30
2. **Zoya Ivanova**, *USSR*   2:34:17
3. **Karolin Szabo**, *Hungary*   2:34:57

In the inaugural World Cup marathon, held in Hiroshima, Japan, the medalists in the men's competition registered three of the ten then-fastest times ever. Another indication of the depth of the field was the 2:11:48 performance of first-American Dean Matthews, good for only thirteenth place. Katrin Doerre, only twenty-three, won her sixth consecutive international marathon. The second IAAF World Cup marathon will be held in Seoul, South Korea in 1987 over the 1988 Olympic Games course.

European Championships

1934 Turin, Italy

1. **Armas Toivonen**, *Finland*   2:52:29.0
2. **Thore Enochsson**, *Sweden*   2:54:35.6
3. **Aurelio Genghini**, *Italy*   2:55:03.4

Armas Toivonen, the 1932 Olympic bronze medalist, passed Thore Enochsson at 30 kilometers and held the lead to win the inaugural European Championships over a 42.750-kilometer course.

1938 Paris, France

1. **Vaino Muinonen**, *Finland*   2:37:28.8
2. **Squire Yarrow**, *Great Britain*   2:39:03.0
3. **Henry Palme**, *Sweden*   2:42:13.6

Vaino Muinonen overtook Squire Yarrow at 35 kilometers and raced to an easy victory in the second European Championships.

1946 Oslo, Norway

1. **Mikko Hietanen**, *Finland*   2:24:55
2. **Vaino Muinonen**, *Finland*   2:26:08
3. **Yakov Punko**, *USSR*   2:26:21

In the first post-war race, and the first with an entry from Russia, forty-seven year old Vaino Muinonen, the winner of the event eight years earlier, finished a creditable second over the 40.2-kilometer course. A Finnish runner won for the third straight time.

1950 Brussels, Belgium

1. **Jack Holden**, *Great Britain*   2:32:13.2
2. **Veikko Karvonen**, *Finland*   2:32:45.0
3. **Feodosiy Vanin**, *USSR*   2:33:47.0

Veikko Karvonen, who almost made it four in a row for the Finns, came from behind to take second place from Feodosiy Vanin by one minute, two seconds, as British Commonwealth champion Jack Holden won by half a minute.

1954 Berne, Switzerland

1. **Veikko Karvonen**, *Finland*   2:24:51.6
2. **Boris Grishayev**, *USSR*   2:24:55.6
3. **Ivan Filin**, *USSR*   2:25:26.6

Ivan Filin, the leader entering the stadium, turned the wrong way on the track and was passed by both Veikko Karvonen, the silver medalist four years earlier, and teammate Boris Grishayev before he figured the way to the tape.

1958 Stockholm, Sweden

1. **Sergey Popov**, *USSR*   2:15:17.0
2. **Ivan Filin**, *USSR*   2:20:50.6
3. **Fred Norris**, *Great Britain*   2:21:15.0

Sergey Popov smashed Jim Peters' 1954 world record by more than two minutes and had the biggest winning margin—over five-and-a-half minutes—in the history of the European Championships.

1962 Belgrade, Yugoslavia

1. **Brian Kilby**, *Great Britain*   2:23:18.8
2. **Aurele Vandendriessche**, *Belgium*   2:24:02.0
3. **Viktor Baikov**, *USSR*   2:24:19.8

Brian Kilby became the second and last marathoner to take both the Commonwealth Games and European Championships in the same year (Jack Holden was the first in 1950).

1966 Budapest, Hungary

1. **Jim Hogan**, *Great Britain*   2:20:04.6
2. **Aurele Vandendriessche**, *Belgium*   2:21:43.6
3. **Gyula Toth**, *Hungary*   2:22:02.0

Jim Hogan took the lead for good at 40 kilometers as Aurele Vandendriessche gained his second silver medal in a row.

1969 Athens, Greece

1. **Ron Hill**, *Great Britain*   2:16:47.8
2. **Gaston Roelants**, *Belgium*   2:17:22.2
3. **Jim Alder**, *Great Britain*   2:19:05.8

Ron Hill passed Gaston Roelants on their approach to the stadium to give Great Britain its third successive victory.

1971 Helsinki, Finland

1. **Karel Lismont**, *Belgium*   2:13:09.0
2. **Trevor Wright**, *Great Britain*   2:13:59.6
3. **Ron Hill**, *Great Britain*   2:14:34.8

Karel Lismont, who went on to win a silver medal in the 1972 Olympics, won by nearly a minute as Ron Hill, the winner two years earlier, came in third.

1974 Rome, Italy

1. **Ian Thompson**, *Great Britain*   2:13:18.8
2. **Eckhard Lesse**, *East Germany*   2:14:57.4
3. **Gaston Roelants**, *Belgium*   2:16:29.6

Unbeaten Ian Thompson, running in his fourth marathon in eleven months, took the lead at the halfway point and romped home to an easy victory. Gaston Roelants, second in 1969 and fifth in 1971, came in third.

1978 Prague, Czechoslovakia

1. **Leonid Moseyev**, *USSR*   2:11:57.5
2. **Nikolay Penzin**, *USSR*   2:11:59.0
3. **Karel Lismont**, *Belgium*   2:12:07.4

Teammates Leonid Moseyev and Nikolay Penzin sprinted to the finish line side by side, with Moseyev edging Penzin at the tape by one-and-a-half seconds, then the closest margin ever in a major championship marathon.

1982 Athens, Greece
Men

1. **Gerard Nijboer**, *Netherlands*   2:15:16
2. **Armand Parmentier**, *Belgium*   2:15:51
3. **Karel Lismont**, *Belgium*   2:16:04

European record-holder Gerard Nijboer took the lead at 27 kilometers and hung on to win as Karel Lismont, the gold medalist eleven years earlier, took third place for the second successive time.

Women

1. **Rosa Mota**, *Portugal*   2:36:04
2. **Laura Fogli**, *Italy*   2:36:29
3. **Ingrid Kristiansen**, *Norway*   2:36:39

In the first women's competition, Rosa Mota, running her first marathon, came in first, while future world-record holder Ingrid Kristiansen finished a close third.

1986 Stuttgart, West Germany
Men

1. **Gelindo Bordin**, *Italy*   2:10:54
2. **Orlando Pizzolato**, *Italy*   2:10:57
3. **Herbert Steffny**, *West Germany*   2:11:30

Great Britain's Steve Jones led the race for the first half, running a 2:06:00 world record marathon pace. However, when he faded, the battle between two Italians provided all the drama. Inside the stadium, with a mere 250 yards to go, unheralded Gelindo Bordin passed two-time New York City Marathon winner Orlando Pizzolato for the victory.

Women

1. **Rosa Mota**, *Portugal*   2:28:38
2. **Laura Fogli**, *Italy*   2:32:52
3. **Yekaterina Khramenkova**, *USSR*   2:34:18

Duplicating her win four years earlier, Rosa Mota won the European Championship marathon for women. This time she was no surprise. The world's third fastest woman marathoner led from the start, once again followed at the finish by Laura Fogli.

European Nations Cup
Men
1981 Agen, France

1. **Massimo Magnani**, *Italy*   2:13:29
2. **Waldemar Cierpinski**, *East Germany*   2:15:44
3. **Tommy Persson**, *Sweden*   2:15:45

1983 Laredo, Spain

1. **Waldemar Cierpinski**, *East Germany*   2:12:26
2. **Jurgen Eberding**, *East Germany*   2:12:26
3. **Gianni Poli**, *Italy*   2:12:28

1985 Rome, Italy

1. **Michael Heilmann**, *East Germany*   2:11:28
2. **Jacques Lefrand**, *France*   2:14:16
3. **Joerg Peter**, *East Germany*   2:14:27

Massimo Magnani took the lead at 30 kilometers in the inaugural European Nations Cup marathon and pulled away to an easy victory. In the second Cup marathon, however, Waldemar Cierpinski, the two-time Olympic champion, barely edged teammate Jurgen Eberding and Gianni Poli after all three sprinted furiously to the tape. The third Cup marathon was similar to the first as Michael Heilmann won comfortably by nearly three minutes in record time.

Women
1981 Agen, France

1. **Zoya Ivanova**, *USSR*   2:38:58
2. **Charlotte Teske**, *West Germany*   2:41:04
3. **Nadyezhda Gumerova**, *USSR*   2:44:49

1983 Laredo, Spain

1. **Nadyezhda Gumerova**, *USSR*   2:38:36
2. **Tamara Surotsyeva**, *USSR*   2:39:17
3. **Raisa Sadryedinova**, *USSR*   2:40:22

1985 Rome, Italy

1. **Katrin Doerre**, *East Germany*   2:30:11
2. **Gabriele Martins**, *East Germany*   2:32:23
3. **Brigit Weinhold**, *East Germany*   2:33:36

Russian runners dominated the first two women's European Nations Cup marathons. But in the third Cup marathon, the best Russian finisher came in fourth, while East Germans—led by Katrin Doerre, the World Cup winner earlier in the year—swept the first three places.

Commonwealth Games
1930 Hamilton, Ontario, Canada

1. **Duncan McLeod Wright**, *Scotland*   2:43:43
2. **Sam Ferris**, *England*   no time
3. **John Miles**, *Canada*   no time

Duncan McLeod Wright took the lead at the 10-mile mark and defeated Sam Ferris by half a mile as John Miles, the Boston Marathon winner in 1926 and 1929, came in third.

The location is London's Westminster Bridge finish but the marathon's message is universal: mankind is a hopeful traveler, a species given to the exploration of its limits.

1934 London, England

1. **Harold Webster**, *Canada*   2:40:36
2. **Donald McNab Robertson**, *Scotland*   2:45:08
3. **Duncan McLeod Wright**, *Scotland*   2:56:20

Duncan McLeod Wright, the winner of the first Commonwealth Games marathon, finished a distant third, while Harold Webster defeated Donald McNab Robertson by over four minutes.

1938 Sydney, Australia

1. **Johannes Coleman**, *South Africa*   2:30:49.8
2. **Bert Norris**, *England*   2:37:57.0
3. **Jack Gibson**, *South Africa*   2:38:20.0

South African runners entered the Commonwealth Games marathon for the first time and took first and third place, with Johannes Coleman winning easily by over seven minutes.

1950 Auckland, New Zealand

1. **Jack Holden**, *England*   2:32:57.0
2. **Sidney Luyt**, *South Africa*   2:37:02.2
3. **Jack Clarke**, *New Zealand*   2:39:26.4

British champion Jack Holden easily won despite having to discard his shoes and run barefoot the last 10 miles, and having to ward off an overzealous dog the last two miles.

1954 Vancouver, British Columbia, Canada

1. **Joe McGhee**, *Scotland*   2:39:36.0
2. **Jack Meckler**, *South Africa*   2:40:57.0
3. **Johannes Barnard**, *South Africa*   2:51:49.8

All the drama of this race revolved around a runner who did not finish. On a scorching-hot August day, world-record holder Jim Peters of England entered the stadium twenty minutes ahead of the field. Suddenly, with victory just ahead of him, he stumbled and fell. Suffering from severe heat exhaustion, Peters wobbled crazily toward the tape 300 yards away. He never made it and was carried unconscious from the track. Only six of the twelve starters finished the race, led by Joe McGhee, who had rested along the way.

1958 Cardiff, Wales

1. **Dave Power**, *Australia*   2:22:45.6
2. **Johannes Barnard**, *South Africa*   2:22:57.4
3. **Peter Wilkinson**, *England*   2:24:42.0

Johannes Barnard, the bronze medalist four years earlier, almost caught Dave Power, who had led from the halfway mark, but fell short by less than twelve seconds.

1962 Perth, Australia

1. **Brian Kilby**, *England*   2:21:17.0
2. **Dave Power**, *Australia*   2:22:15.4
3. **Rod Bonella**, *Australia*   2:24:07.0

European Games champion Brian Kilby gained the lead at 30 kilometers and edged Dave Power, the winner four years earlier.

1966 Kingston, Jamaica

1. **Jim Alder**, *Scotland*   2:22:07.8
2. **Bill Adcocks**, *England*   2:22:13.0
3. **Mike Ryan**, *New Zealand*   2:27:59.0

Jim Alder, the leader from the 20-mile mark, was misdirected as he entered the stadium and Bill Adcocks quickly took over the lead. But Alder had enough left to beat Adcocks to the tape.

1970 Edinburgh, Scotland

1. **Ron Hill**, *England*   2:09:28
2. **Jim Alder**, *Scotland*   2:12:04
3. **Don Faircloth**, *England*   2:12:19

Ron Hill led a strong field through the halfway mark in a record 1:02:35.2 and went on to set a British and European record time as he won by two-and-a-half minutes over Jim Alder, the gold medalist four years earlier.

Carlos Lopes happily hoists the flag of Portugal after winning the concluding event of the 1984 Olympic Games in Los Angeles.

1974 Christchurch, New Zealand

1. **Ian Thompson**, *England*   2:09:12.0
2. **Jack Foster**, *New Zealand*   2:11:18.6
3. **Richard Mabuza**, *Swaziland*   2:12:54.4

Ian Thompson, running only his second marathon, clipped sixteen seconds off Ron Hill's Commonwealth Games marathon mark as Hill finished eighteenth.

1978 Edmonton, Alberta, Canada

1. **Gidamis Shahanga**, *Tanzania*   2:15:39.8
2. **Jerome Drayton**, *Canada*   2:16:13.5
3. **Paul Bannon**, *Canada*   2:16:51.6

Unknown Gidamis Shahanga passed Jerome Drayton just outside the stadium to become the first black African to win the Commonwealth Games marathon.

1982 Brisbane, Australia

1. **Robert de Castella**, *Australia*   2:09:18
2. **Juma Ikangaa**, *Tanzania*   2:09:30
3. **Mike Gratton**, *England*   2:12:06

Robert de Castella caught Juma Ikangaa at 40 kilometers and the two alternated in the lead until de Castella pulled away to win by only twelve seconds.

1986 Edinburgh, Scotland
Men

1. **Robert de Castella**, *Australia*   2:10:15
2. **David Edge**, *Canada*   2:11:08
3. **Steve Moneghetti**, *Australia*   2:11:18

Women

1. **Lisa Martin**, *Australia*   2:26:07
2. **Lorraine Moller**, *New Zealand*   2:28:17
3. **Odette Lapierre**, *Canada*   2:31:48

Four months after winning the Boston Marathon in history's third-fastest time (2:07:51), Robert de Castella easily became the first repeat winner of the Commonwealth Games marathon. Another innovation was a marathon race for women. De Castella was the first to congratulate teammate Lisa Martin as she finished far ahead of rival Lorraine Moller of New Zealand. The Games were diminished when thirty-two of the fifty-eight Commonwealth nations stayed home in protest of England's refusal to impose economic sanctions against South Africa.

Pan American Games
1951 Buenos Aires, Argentina

1. **Delfo Cabrera**, *Argentina*   2:35:00.2
2. **Reinaldo Gorno**, *Argentina*   2:45:00.0
3. **Luis Velazquez**, *Guatemala*   2:46:02.8

The 1948 Olympic champion, Delfo Cabrera, breezed to an easy victory in the inaugural Pan American Games marathon by almost exactly ten minutes, the biggest margin ever in a major marathon.

1955 Mexico City, Mexico

1. **Doroteo Flores**, *Guatemala*   2:59:09.2
2. **Onesimo Rodriguez**, *Mexico*   3:02:25.6
3. **Luis Velazquez**, *Guatemala*   3:05:25.2

Inexperience in running at high altitudes created unusually poor times—Doroteo Flores, the 1952 Boston Marathon winner, was the only runner to break three hours. Undaunted, Luis Velazquez finished third for the second time in a row.

1959 Chicago, Illinois

1. **John J. Kelley**, *USA*   2:27:54.2
2. **Jim Green**, *USA*   2:32:16.9
3. **Gordon Dickson**, *Canada*   2:36:18.6

John J. Kelley, the 1957 Boston Marathon champion, led the US to its best Pan American Games marathon showing as American runners came in first, second, and fourth.

1963 São Paulo, Brazil

1. **Fidel Negrete**, *Mexico*   2:27:55.6
2. **Gordon McKenzie**, *USA*   2:31:17.2
3. **Peter McArdle**, *USA*   2:34:14.0

Fidel Negrete, who would come in twenty-first in the 1964 Olympic marathon, set a national record in beating two of America's best marathoners.

1967 Winnipeg, Manitoba, Canada

1. **Andy Boychuk**, *Canada*   2:23:02.4
2. **Agustin Calle**, *Colombia*   2:25:50.2
3. **Alfredo Penaloza**, *Mexico*   2:27:48.2

Andy Boychuk's victory made Canada the fifth winning nation in the first five Pan American Games marathons.

1971 Cali, Colombia

1. **Frank Shorter**, *USA*   2:22:40
2. **Jose Gaspar**, *Mexico*   2:26:30
3. **Hernan Barreneche**, *Colombia*   2:27:19

Frank Shorter, the 1972 Olympic Games marathon gold medalist, would become the second Olympic champion to win the Pan American Games marathon.

1975 Mexico City, Mexico

1. **Rigoberto Mendoza**, *Cuba*   2:25:02.9
2. **Chuck Smead**, *USA*   2:25:31.6
3. **Tom Howard**, *Canada*   2:25:45.5

High altitude again bothered the marathoners as Rigoberto Mendoza overtook Chuck Smead and Tom Howard, the leaders for most of the race, to win in the closest finish in the history of the Pan American Games marathon.

1979 San Juan, Puerto Rico

1. **Radames Gonzalez**, *Cuba*   2:24:09
2. **Luis Barbosa**, *Colombia*   2:24:44
3. **Rick Hughson**, *Canada*   2:25:34

Radames Gonzalez gave Cuba its second victory in succession in a narrow win over Luis Barbosa.

1983 Caracas, Venezuela

1. **Jorge Gonzalez**, *Puerto Rico*   2:12:42
2. **Cesar Mercado**, *Puerto Rico*   2:20:29
3. **Miguel Cruz**, *Mexico*   2:21:11

Jose Gonzalez set a Pan American Games marathon record as he defeated teammate Cesar Mercado by nearly eight minutes. The 1987 Pan American Games will take place in Indianapolis, Indiana, and will include a marathon for women.

The Big Four

By the mid-1980s, four annual races towered above all the rest of the world's five hundred marathons in both riches and prestige. The Boston Marathon and the London Marathon competed each spring for the top runners, while America's Marathon/Chicago and the New York City Marathon followed suit in the fall. The Big Four produced six of the ten fastest times run by men and nine of the top ten fastest times run by women, including Ingrid Kristiansen's world record (2:21:06, London 1985). These four races were each able to assemble multimillion-dollar budgets and dispense some $250,000 in prize money.

The Big Four also have unique offerings for the masses of amateurs. New York has the most dramatic start in marathoning (the Verrazano-Narrows Bridge); London has the most scenic finish (Buckingham Palace, the Houses of Parliament, Big Ben, and Westminster Bridge); Chicago has the most supportive sponsor (Beatrice Companies, Inc.); and Boston has the most tradition (the race began in 1897).

Boston Marathon
Men

Year	Winner	Time
1897	John J. McDermott, USA	2:55:10
1898	Ronald J. McDonald, USA	2:42:00
1899	Lawrence J. Brignolia, USA	2:54:38
1900	James J. Caffrey, Canada	2:39:44
1901	James J. Caffrey, Canada	2:29:23
1902	Samuel A. Mellor, USA	2:43:12
1903	John C. Lorden, USA	2:41:29
1904	Michael Spring, USA	2:38:04
1905	Fred Lord, USA	2:38:25
1906	Timothy Ford, USA	2:45:45
1907	Thomas Longboat, Canada	2:24:24
1908	Thomas P. Morrissey, USA	2:25:43
1909	Henri Renaud, USA	2:53:36
1910	Fred L. Cameron, Canada	2:28:52
1911	Clarence H. DeMar, USA	2:21:39
1912	Michael J. Ryan, USA	2:21:18
1913	Fritz Carlson, USA	2:25:14
1914	James Duffy, Canada	2:25:01
1915	Edouard Fabre, Canada	2:31:41
1916	Arthur V. Roth, USA	2:27:16
1917	William K. Kennedy, USA	2:28:37
1918	(WWI Service Team Race won by Camp Devens)	
1919	Carl W. A. Linder, USA	2:29:13
1920	Peter Trivoulidas, Greece	2:29:31
1921	Frank Zuna, USA	2:18:57
1922	Clarence H. DeMar, USA	2:18:10
1923	Clarence H. DeMar, USA	2:23:37
1924	Clarence H. DeMar, USA	2:29:40
1925	Charles L. Mellor, USA	2:33:00
1926	John C. Miles, Canada	2:25:40
1927	Clarence H. DeMar, USA	2:40:22
1928	Clarence H. DeMar, USA	2:37:07
1929	John C. Miles, Canada	2:33:08
1930	Clarence H. DeMar, USA	2:34:48
1931	James P. Henigan, USA	2:46:45
1932	Paul de Bruyn, Germany	2:33:36
1933	Leslie Pawson, USA	2:31:01
1934	Dave Komonen, Canada	2:32:53
1935	John A. Kelley, USA	2:32:07
1936	Ellison M. "Tarzan" Brown, USA	2:33:40
1937	Walter Young, Canada	2:33:20
1938	Leslie Pawson, USA	2:35:34
1939	Ellison M. "Tarzan" Brown, USA	2:28:51
1940	Gerard Cote, Canada	2:28:25
1941	Leslie Pawson, USA	2:30:38
1942	Bernard Joe Smith, USA	2:26:51
1943	Gerard Cote, Canada	2:28:25
1944	Gerard Cote, Canada	2:31:50
1945	John A. Kelley, USA	2:30:40
1946	Stylianos Kyriakides, Greece	2:29:27
1947	Yun Bok Suh, Korea	2:25:39*
1948	Gerard Cote, Canada	2:31:02
1949	Karle Gosta Leandersson, Sweden	2:31:50
1950	Kee Yong Ham, Korea	2:32:39
1951	Shigeki Tanaka, Japan	2:27:45
1952	Doroteo Flores, Guatemala	2:31:53
1953	Keizo Yamada, Japan	2:18:51
1954	Veikko L. Karvonen, Finland	2:20:39
1955	Hideo Hamamura, Japan	2:18:22
1956	Antti Viskari, Finland	2:14:14
1957	John J. Kelley, USA	2:20:05
1958	Franjo Mihalic, Yugoslavia	2:25:54
1959	Eino Oksanen, Finland	2:22:42
1960	Paavo Kotila, Finland	2:20:54
1961	Eino Oksanen, Finland	2:23:39
1962	Eino Oksanen, Finland	2:23:48
1963	Aurele Vandendriessche, Belgium	2:18:58
1964	Aurele Vandendriessche, Belgium	2:19:59
1965	Morio Shigematsu, Japan	2:16:33
1966	Kenji Kimihara, Japan	2:17:11
1967	David McKenzie, New Zealand	2:15:45
1968	Ambrose Burfoot, USA	2:22:17
1969	Yoshiaki Unetani, Japan	2:13:49
1970	Ron Hill, Great Britain	2:10:30
1971	Alavaro Mejia, USA	2:18:45
1972	Olavi Suomalainen, Finland	2:15:39
1973	Jon Anderson, USA	2:16:03
1974	Neil Cusack, USA	2:13:39
1975	Bill Rodgers, USA	2:09:55
1976	Jack Fultz, USA	2:20:19
1977	Jerome Drayton, Canada	2:14:46
1978	Bill Rodgers, USA	2:10:13
1979	Bill Rodgers, USA	2:09:27
1980	Bill Rodgers, USA	2:12:11
1981	Toshihiko Seko, Japan	2:09:26

1982 Alberto Salazar, USA	2:08:52**
1983 Greg Meyer, USA	2:09:00
1984 Geoff Smith, Great Britain	2:10:34
1985 Geoff Smith, Great Britain	2:14:05
1986 Robert de Castella, Australia	2:07:51

Women

1972 Nina Kuscsik, USA	3:10:26
1973 Jacqueline Hansen, USA	3:05:59
1974 Miki Gorman, USA	2:47:11
1975 Liane Winter, West Germany	2:42:24*
1976 Kim Merritt, USA	2:47:10
1977 Miki Gorman, USA	2:46:22
1978 Gayle Barron, USA	2:44:52
1979 Joan Benoit, USA	2:35:15
1980 Jacqueline Gareau, Canada	2:34:28
1981 Allison Roe, New Zealand	2:26:46
1982 Charlotte Teske, West Germany	2:29:33
1983 Joan Benoit, USA	2:22:43**
1984 Lorraine Moller, New Zealand	2:29:28
1985 Lisa Larsen Weidenbach, USA	2:34:06
1986 Ingrid Kristiansen, Norway	2:24:55

*Former world record.   **American record.

America's Marathon/Chicago
Men

1977 Dan Cloeter, USA	2:17:52
1978 Mark Stanforth, USA	2:19:20
1979 Dan Cloeter, USA	2:23:20
1980 Frank Richardson, USA	2:14:04
1981 Phil Coppess, USA	2:16:13
1982 Greg Meyer, USA	2:10:59
1983 Joe Nzau, Kenya	2:09:45
1984 Steve Jones, Great Britain	2:08:05*
1985 Steve Jones, Great Britain	2:07:13
1986 Toshihiko Seko, Japan	2:08:27

Women

1977 Dorothy Doolittle, USA	2:50:47
1978 Lynae Larson, USA	2:59:00
1979 Lorna Michalak, USA	3:15:45
1980 Sue Peterson, USA	2:45:03
1981 Tina Gandy, USA	2:47:37
1982 Nancy Conz, USA	2:33:23
1983 Rosa Mota, Portugal	2:31:12
1984 Rosa Mota, Portugal	2:26:01
1985 Joan Benoit Samuelson, USA	2:21:21**
1986 Ingrid Kristiansen, Norway	2:27:08

*Former world record.   **American record.

London Marathon
Men

1981 Dick Beardsley, USA	2:11:48
Inge Simonsen, Norway	2:11:48
1982 Hugh Jones, Great Britain	2:09:24

1983 Mike Gratton, Great Britain	2:09:43
1984 Charlie Spedding, Great Britain	2:09:57
1985 Steve Jones, Great Britain	2:08:16
1986 Toshihiko Seko, Japan	2:10:02

Women

1981 Joyce Smith, Great Britain	2:29:57
1982 Joyce Smith, Great Britain	2:29:43
1983 Grete Waitz, Norway	2:25:29*
1984 Ingrid Kristiansen, Norway	2:24:26
1985 Ingrid Kristiansen, Norway	2:21:06***
1986 Grete Waitz, Norway	2:24:54

*Former world record.   ***World record.

New York City Marathon
Men

1970 Gary Muhrcke, USA	2:31:38.2
1971 Norman Higgins, USA	2:22:54.2
1972 Sheldon Karlin, USA	2:27:52.8
1973 Tom Fleming, USA	2:21:54.8
1974 Norbert Sander, USA	2:26:30.2
1975 Tom Fleming, USA	2:19:27
1976 Bill Rodgers, USA	2:10:09.6
1977 Bill Rodgers, USA	2:11:28.2
1978 Bill Rodgers, USA	2:12:12
1979 Bill Rodgers, USA	2:11:42
1980 Alberto Salazar, USA	2:09:41
1981 Alberto Salazar, USA	2:08:13**
1982 Alberto Salazar, USA	2:09:29
1983 Rod Dixon, New Zealand	2:08:59
1984 Orlando Pizzolato, Italy	2:14:53
1985 Orlando Pizzolato, Italy	2:11:34
1986 Gianni Poli, Italy	2:11:06

Women

1970 No finisher	
1971 Beth Bonner, USA	2:55:22
1972 Nina Kuscsik, USA	3:08:41.6
1973 Nina Kuscsik, USA	2:57:07.2
1974 Katherine Switzer, USA	3:07:29
1975 Kim Merritt, USA	2:46:14.8
1976 Miki Gorman, USA	2:39:11
1977 Miki Gorman, USA	2:43:10
1978 Grete Waitz, Norway	2:32:30*
1979 Grete Waitz, Norway	2:27:33*
1980 Grete Waitz, Norway	2:25:41*
1981 Allison Roe, New Zealand	2:25:29**
1982 Grete Waitz, Norway	2:27:14
1983 Grete Waitz, Norway	2:27:00
1984 Grete Waitz, Norway	2:29:30
1985 Grete Waitz, Norway	2:28:34
1986 Grete Waitz, Norway	2:28:06

*Former world record.

**World record not officially recognized.

PACE CHART

Mile Pace	5K (3.1M)	5 Miles	10K (6.2M)	15K (9.3M)	10 Miles	20K (12.4M)	Half Marathon	15 Miles	25K (15.5M)	30K (18.6M)	20 Miles	35K (21.7M)	40K (24.8M)	Full Marathon
4:40	14:30	23:20	29:00	43:30	46:40	58:00	1:01:11	1:10:00	1:12:30	1:27:00	1:33:20	1:41:30	1:56:00	2:02:22
4:45	14:46	23:45	29:31	44:17	47:30	59:02	1:02:17	1:11:15	1:13:48	1:28:33	1:35:00	1:43:19	1:58:04	2:04:33
4:50	15:01	24:10	30:02	45:03	48:20	1:00:04	1:03:22	1:12:30	1:15:05	1:30:06	1:36:40	1:45:07	2:00:08	2:06:44
4:55	15:17	24:35	30:33	45:50	49:10	1:01:06	1:04:28	1:13:45	1:16:23	1:31:39	1:38:20	1:46:56	2:02:12	2:08:55
5:00	15:32	25:00	31:04	46:36	50:00	1:02:08	1:05:33	1:15:00	1:17:40	1:33:12	1:40:00	1:48:44	2:04:16	2:11:06
5:05	15:48	25:25	31:35	47:23	50:50	1:03:10	1:06:39	1:16:15	1:18:58	1:34:45	1:41:40	1:50:33	2:06:20	2:13:17
5:10	16:03	25:50	32:06	48:09	51:40	1:04:12	1:07:44	1:17:30	1:20:15	1:36:18	1:43:20	1:52:21	2:08:24	2:15:28
5:15	16:19	26:15	32:37	48:56	52:30	1:05:14	1:08:50	1:18:45	1:21:33	1:37:51	1:45:00	1:54:10	2:10:28	2:17:39
5:20	16:34	26:40	33:08	49:42	53:20	1:06:16	1:09:55	1:20:00	1:22:50	1:39:24	1:46:40	1:55:58	2:12:32	2:19:50
5:25	16:50	27:05	33:39	50:29	54:10	1:07:18	1:11:01	1:21:15	1:24:08	1:40:57	1:48:20	1:57:47	2:14:36	2:22:01
5:30	17:05	27:30	34:10	51:15	55:00	1:08:20	1:12:06	1:22:30	1:25:25	1:42:30	1:50:00	1:59:35	2:16:40	2:24:12
5:35	17:21	27:55	34:41	52:02	55:50	1:09:22	1:13:12	1:23:45	1:26:43	1:44:03	1:51:40	2:01:24	2:18:44	2:26:23
5:40	17:36	28:20	35:12	52:48	56:40	1:10:24	1:14:17	1:25:00	1:28:00	1:45:36	1:53:20	2:03:12	2:20:48	2:28:34
5:45	17:52	28:45	35:43	53:35	57:30	1:11:26	1:15:23	1:26:15	1:29:18	1:47:09	1:55:00	2:05:01	2:22:52	2:30:45
5:50	18:07	29:10	36:14	54:21	58:20	1:12:28	1:16:28	1:27:30	1:30:35	1:48:42	1:56:40	2:06:49	2:24:56	2:32:56
5:55	18:23	29:35	36:45	55:08	59:10	1:13:30	1:17:34	1:28:45	1:31:53	1:50:15	1:58:20	2:08:38	2:27:00	2:35:07
6:00	18:38	30:00	37:16	55:54	1:00:00	1:14:32	1:18:39	1:30:00	1:33:10	1:51:48	2:00:00	2:10:26	2:29:04	2:37:18
6:05	18:54	30:25	37:47	56:41	1:00:50	1:15:34	1:19:45	1:31:15	1:34:28	1:53:21	2:01:40	2:12:15	2:31:08	2:39:29
6:10	19:09	30:50	38:18	57:27	1:01:40	1:16:36	1:20:50	1:32:30	1:35:45	1:54:54	2:03:20	2:14:03	2:33:12	2:41:40
6:15	19:25	31:15	38:49	58:14	1:02:30	1:17:38	1:21:56	1:33:45	1:37:03	1:56:27	2:05:00	2:15:52	2:35:16	2:43:51
6:20	19:40	31:40	39:20	59:00	1:03:20	1:18:40	1:23:01	1:35:00	1:38:20	1:58:00	2:06:40	2:17:40	2:37:20	2:46:02
6:25	19:56	32:05	39:51	59:47	1:04:10	1:19:42	1:24:07	1:36:15	1:39:38	1:59:33	2:08:20	2:19:29	2:39:24	2:48:13
6:30	20:11	32:30	40:22	1:00:33	1:05:00	1:20:44	1:25:12	1:37:30	1:40:55	2:01:06	2:10:00	2:21:17	2:41:28	2:50:24
6:35	20:27	32:55	40:53	1:01:20	1:05:50	1:21:46	1:26:18	1:38:45	1:42:13	2:02:39	2:11:40	2:23:06	2:43:32	2:52:35
6:40	20:42	33:20	41:24	1:02:06	1:06:40	1:22:48	1:27:23	1:40:00	1:43:30	2:04:12	2:13:20	2:24:54	2:45:36	2:54:46
6:45	20:58	33:45	41:55	1:02:53	1:07:30	1:23:50	1:28:29	1:41:15	1:44:48	2:05:45	2:15:00	2:26:43	2:47:40	2:56:57
6:50	21:13	34:10	42:26	1:03:39	1:08:20	1:24:52	1:29:34	1:42:30	1:46:05	2:07:18	2:16:40	2:28:31	2:49:44	2:59:08
6:55	21:29	34:35	42:57	1:04:26	1:09:10	1:25:54	1:30:40	1:43:45	1:47:23	2:08:51	2:18:20	2:30:20	2:51:48	3:01:19
7:00	21:44	35:00	43:28	1:05:12	1:10:00	1:26:56	1:31:45	1:45:00	1:48:40	2:10:24	2:20:00	2:32:08	2:53:52	3:03:30
7:05	30:00	35:25	43:59	1:05:59	1:10:50	1:27:58	1:32:51	1:46:15	1:49:58	2:11:57	2:21:40	2:33:57	2:55:56	3:05:41
7:10	22:15	35:50	44:30	1:06:45	1:11:40	1:29:00	1:33:56	1:47:30	1:51:15	2:13:30	2:23:20	2:35:45	2:58:00	3:07:52
7:15	22:31	36:15	45:01	1:07:32	1:12:30	1:30:02	1:35:02	1:48:45	1:52:33	2:15:03	2:25:00	2:37:34	3:00:04	3:10:03
7:20	22:46	36:40	45:32	1:08:18	1:13:20	1:31:04	1:36:07	1:50:00	1:53:50	2:16:36	2:26:40	2:39:22	3:02:08	3:12:14
7:25	23:02	37:05	46:03	1:09:05	1:14:10	1:32:06	1:37:13	1:51:15	1:55:08	2:18:09	2:28:20	2:41:11	3:04:12	3:14:25
7:30	23:17	35:30	46:34	1:09:51	1:15:00	1:33:08	1:38:18	1:52:30	1:56:25	2:19:42	2:30:00	2:42:59	3:06:16	3:16:36
7:35	23:33	37:55	47:05	1:10:38	1:15:50	1:34:10	1:39:24	1:53:45	1:57:43	2:21:15	2:31:40	2:44:48	3:08:20	3:18:47
7:40	23:48	38:20	47:36	1:11:24	1:16:40	1:35:12	1:40:29	1:55:00	1:59:00	2:22:48	2:33:20	2:46:36	3:10:24	3:20:58
7:45	24:04	38:45	48:07	1:12:11	1:17:30	1:36:14	1:41:35	1:56:15	2:00:18	2:24:21	2:35:00	2:48:25	3:12:28	3:23:09
7:50	24:19	39:10	48:38	1:12:57	1:18:20	1:37:16	1:42:40	1:57:30	2:01:35	2:25:54	2:36:40	2:50:13	3:14:32	3:25:20

8:00	24:50	40:00		1:14:50	1:20:00	1:39:20					2:40:00		3:18:40	
8:05	25:06	40:25	50:11	1:15:17	1:20:50	1:40:22	1:45:57	2:01:15	2:05:28	2:30:33	2:41:40	2:55:29	3:20:44	3:31:53
8:10	25:21	40:50	50:42	1:16:03	1:21:40	1:41:24	1:47:02	2:02:30	2:06:45	2:32:06	2:43:20	2:57:27	3:22:48	3:34:04
8:15	25:37	41:15	51:13	1:16:50	1:22:30	1:42:26	1:48:08	2:03:45	2:08:03	2:33:39	2:45:00	2:59:16	3:24:52	3:36:15
8:20	25:52	41:40	51:44	1:17:36	1:23:20	1:43:28	1:49:13	2:05:00	2:09:20	2:35:12	2:46:40	3:01:04	3:26:56	3:38:26
8:25	26:08	42:05	52:15	1:18:23	1:24:10	1:44:30	1:50:19	2:06:15	2:10:38	2:36:45	2:48:20	3:02:53	3:29:00	3:40:37
8:30	26:23	42:30	52:46	1:19:09	1:25:00	1:45:32	1:51:24	2:07:30	2:11:55	2:38:18	2:50:00	3:04:41	3:31:04	3:42:48
8:35	26:39	42:55	53:17	1:19:56	1:25:50	1:46:34	1:52:30	2:08:45	2:13:13	2:39:51	2:51:40	3:06:30	3:33:08	3:44:59
8:40	26:54	43:20	53:48	1:20:42	1:26:40	1:47:36	1:53:35	2:10:00	2:14:30	2:41:24	2:53:20	3:08:18	3:35:12	3:47:10
8:45	27:10	43:45	54:19	1:21:29	1:27:30	1:48:38	1:54:41	2:11:15	2:15:48	2:42:57	2:55:00	3:10:07	3:37:16	3:49:21
8:50	27:25	44:10	54:50	1:22:15	1:28:20	1:49:40	1:55:46	2:12:30	2:17:05	2:44:30	2:56:40	3:11:55	3:39:20	3:51:32
8:55	27:41	44:35	55:21	1:23:02	1:29:10	1:50:42	1:56:52	2:13:45	2:18:23	2:46:03	2:58:20	3:13:44	3:41:24	3:53:43
9:00	27:56	45:00	55:52	1:23:48	1:30:00	1:51:44	1:57:57	2:15:00	2:19:40	2:47:36	3:00:00	3:15:32	3:43:28	3:55:54
9:05	28:12	45:25	56:23	1:24:35	1:30:50	1:52:46	1:59:03	2:16:15	2:20:58	2:49:09	3:01:40	3:17:21	3:45:32	3:58:05
9:10	28:27	45:50	56:54	1:25:21	1:31:40	1:53:48	2:00:08	2:17:30	2:22:15	2:50:42	3:03:20	3:19:09	3:47:36	4:00:16
9:15	28:43	46:15	57:25	1:26:08	1:32:30	1:54:50	2:01:14	2:18:45	2:23:33	2:52:15	3:05:00	3:20:58	3:49:40	4:02:27
9:20	28:58	46:40	57:56	1:26:54	1:33:20	1:55:52	2:02:19	2:20:00	2:24:50	2:53:48	3:06:40	3:22:46	3:51:44	4:04:38
9:25	29:14	47:05	58:27	1:27:41	1:34:10	1:56:54	2:03:25	2:21:15	2:26:08	2:55:21	3:08:20	3:24:35	3:53:48	4:06:49
9:30	29:29	47:30	58:58	1:28:27	1:35:00	1:57:56	2:04:30	2:22:30	2:27:25	2:56:54	3:10:00	3:26:23	3:55:52	4:09:00
9:35	29:45	47:55	59:29	1:29:14	1:35:50	1:58:58	2:05:36	2:23:45	2:28:43	2:58:27	3:11:40	3:28:12	3:57:56	4:11:11
9:40	30:00	48:20	1:00:00	1:30:00	1:36:40	2:00:00	2:06:41	2:25:00	2:30:00	3:00:00	3:13:20	3:30:00	4:00:00	4:13:22
9:45	30:16	48:45	1:00:31	1:30:47	1:37:30	2:01:02	2:07:47	2:26:15	2:31:18	3:01:33	3:15:00	3:31:49	4:02:04	4:15:33
9:50	30:31	49:10	1:01:02	1:31:33	1:38:20	2:02:04	2:08:52	2:27:30	2:32:35	3:03:06	3:16:40	3:33:37	4:04:08	4:17:44
9:55	30:47	49:35	1:01:33	1:32:20	1:39:10	2:03:06	2:09:58	2:28:45	2:33:53	3:04:39	3:18:20	3:35:26	4:06:12	4:19:55
10:00	31:02	50:00	1:02:04	1:33:06	1:40:00	2:04:08	2:11:03	2:30:00	2:35:10	3:06:12	3:20:00	3:37:14	4:08:16	4:22:06
10:05	31:18	50:25	1:02:35	1:33:53	1:40:50	2:05:10	2:12:09	2:31:15	2:36:28	3:07:45	3:21:40	3:39:03	4:10:20	4:24:17
10:10	31:33	50:50	1:03:06	1:34:39	1:41:40	2:06:12	2:13:14	2:32:30	2:37:45	3:09:18	3:23:20	3:40:51	4:12:24	4:26:28
10:15	31:49	51:15	1:03:37	1:35:26	1:42:30	2:07:14	2:14:20	2:33:45	2:39:03	3:10:51	3:25:00	3:42:40	4:14:28	4:28:39
10:20	32:04	51:40	1:04:08	1:36:12	1:43:20	2:08:16	2:15:25	2:35:00	2:40:20	3:12:24	3:26:40	3:44:28	4:16:32	4:30:50
10:25	32:20	52:05	1:04:39	1:36:59	1:44:10	2:09:18	2:16:31	2:36:15	2:41:38	3:13:57	3:28:20	3:46:17	4:18:36	4:33:01
10:30	32:35	52:30	1:05:10	1:37:45	1:45:00	2:10:20	2:17:36	2:37:30	2:42:55	3:15:30	3:30:00	3:48:05	4:20:40	4:35:12
10:35	32:51	52:55	1:05:41	1:38:32	1:45:50	2:11:22	2:18:42	2:38:45	2:44:13	3:17:03	3:31:40	3:49:54	4:22:44	4:37:23
10:40	33:06	53:20	1:06:12	1:39:18	1:46:40	2:12:24	2:19:47	2:40:00	2:45:30	3:18:36	3:33:20	3:51:42	4:24:48	4:39:34
10:45	33:22	53:45	1:06:43	1:40:05	1:47:30	2:13:26	2:20:53	2:41:15	2:46:48	3:20:09	3:35:00	3:53:31	4:26:52	4:41:45
10:50	33:37	54:10	1:07:14	1:40:51	1:48:20	2:14:28	2:21:58	2:42:30	2:48:05	3:21:42	3:36:40	3:55:19	4:28:56	4:43:56
10:55	33:53	54:35	1:07:45	1:41:38	1:49:10	2:15:30	2:23:04	2:43:45	2:49:23	3:23:15	3:38:20	3:57:08	4:31:00	4:46:07
11:00	34:08	55:00	1:08:16	1:42:24	1:50:00	2:16:32	2:24:09	2:45:00	2:50:40	3:24:48	3:40:00	3:58:56	4:33:04	4:48:18
11:05	34:24	55:25	1:08:47	1:43:11	1:50:50	2:17:34	2:25:15	2:46:15	2:51:58	3:26:21	3:41:40	4:00:45	4:35:08	4:50:29
11:10	34:39	55:50	1:09:18	1:43:57	1:51:40	2:18:36	2:26:20	2:47:30	2:53:15	3:27:54	3:43:20	4:02:33	4:37:12	4:52:40
11:15	34:55	56:15	1:09:49	1:44:44	1:52:30	2:19:38	2:27:26	2:48:45	2:54:33	3:29:27	3:45:00	4:04:22	4:39:16	4:54:51
11:20	35:10	56:40	1:10:20	1:45:30	1:53:20	2:20:40	2:28:31	2:50:00	2:55:50	3:31:00	3:46:40	4:06:10	4:41:20	4:57:02
11:25	35:26	57:05	1:10:51	1:46:17	1:54:10	2:21:42	2:29:37	2:51:15	2:57:08	3:32:33	3:48:20	4:07:59	4:43:24	4:59:13
11:30	35:41	57:30	1:11:22	1:47:03	1:55:00	2:22:44	2:30:42	2:52:30	2:58:25	3:34:06	3:50:00	4:09:47	4:45:28	5:01:24

Photo credits

Frontmatter
1: clockwise from top left, © 1981 Ira Wyman, Sygma; © 1985 Maier Media; © 1985 Simon Bruty, All-Sport; © 1984 Tannenbaum, Sygma. Frontispiece: © 1982 Gerard Vandystadt, Agence Vandystadt. Title page: © 1987 L. Krautter.

The Start
8: © 1984 Janeart. 11: © 1983 Tony Feder, Impressions. 12: both, BBC-Hulton Picture Library/The Bettmann Archive. 13: top, UPI/Bettman Newsphotos; bottom, BBC-Hulton Picture Library/ The Bettmann Archives. 14: BBC-Hulton Picture Library/The Bettmann Archive. 15: © Pascal Danot, Agence Vandystadt. 17: top, © 1981 Bill Paciello, Duomo; bottom, © André Lapderrière, courtesy Montreal International Marathon. 18: © 1980 Tracy Frankel, Janeart. 19: © Mike Powell, All-Sport. 20: © 1972 Neil Leifer/*Sports Illustrated.*

The Course
All medals, trophies, and plaques were photographed by Leslie Jean-Bart (except page 43).
22: © Stockholm Marathon. 25: © 1987 Jorn Stjerneklar. 26: © 1987 Sandy Treadwell. 27: © 1987 Jorn Stjerneklar. 28, 29: © 1987 Jorn Stjerneklar. 30: © 1982 Steve Powell, All-Sport. 31: © George Courmouzis. 33: © George Courmouzis. 34: © 1987 Sandy Treadwell. 36: © 1987 Sandy Treadwell. 37: both, © 1982 Kim Studio. 38: © 1983 Peter Nichols. 41: © 1987 Sandy Treadwell.

42: both, © 1987 Sandy Treadwell. 43: © 1987 Sandy Treadwell. 45: © 1985 Bernd Wende. 46, 47: © 1985 Bernd Wende. 50: © 1985 Bernd Wende. 51: © 1985 Bernd Wende. 53: © 1986 Neville Trott, courtesy Bermuda Department of Tourism. 55: © 1986 Neville Trott, courtesy Bermuda Department of Tourism. 56: © 1985 Victor G Sailer, Sailer/McManus. 57: © 1986 Sailer/McManus. 59: © 1975 Neil Leifer. 60: © 1981 Paul J. Sutton, Duomo. 61: © 1981 Ira Wyman, Sygma.

62: © 1985 Paul J. Sutton, Duomo. 63: top, © 1987 Sandy Treadwell; bottom, © 1985 Janeart. 64: © 1985 Paul J. Sutton, Duomo. 66: top, © 1985 Paul J. Sutton, Duomo; bottom, © 1985 Paul J. Sutton, Duomo. 67: © 1987 Sandy Treadwell. 68: © 1987 Sandy Treadwell. 69: courtesy *Irish Runner.* 70: courtesy *Irish Runner.* 73: © 1982 David Madison, Duomo. 75: © 1985 Takashi Ito. 76, 77: © 1985 Takashi Ito. 78: © 1981 Martti Peltonen, Lehtikuva Oy. 81: © 1983 Jiha Jormanainen, Lehtikuva Oy.

82: top, © 1987 Sandy Treadwell; bottom, © 1981 Heikki Kotilainen, Lehtikuva Oy; 83: top, © 1982 Peritti Jenytin, Lehtikuva Oy; bottom, © 1983 Paul J. Sutton, Duomo. 84: © 1985 Richard Edge. 85: © 1985 Richard Edge. 87: both, © 1985 Richard Edge. 88: top, © 1985 Richard Edge; bottom, ©

1987 Sandy Treadwell. 89: top, © 1985 Richard Edge; bottom, © 1987 Sandy Treadwell. 90: © 1985 Simon Miles, All-Sport. 91: © 1985 Simon Miles, All-Sport. 93: © 1983 Mike Allen, All-Sport. 94, 95: © All-Sport. 96: © 1985 Trevor Jones, All-Sport. 97: top, © 1985 Simon Miles, All-Sport; bottom, © 1985 Michael King, All-Sport. 98: © 1983 Tony Feder, Impressions. 99: both, © Tony Feder, Impressions. 101: both, © Tony Feder, Impressions.

102: © 1983 Tony Feder, Impressions. 103: © Impressions. 104: © Entre 2 Design, courtesy Montreal International Marathon. 105: courtesy Montreal International Marathon. 107: courtesy Montreal International Marathon. 108: © Entre 2 Design, courtesy Montreal International Marathon. 110: courtesy Andy Golovanov. 111: © 1979 Tony Duffy, All-Sport. 113: © 1979 Tony Duffy, All-Sport. 114: top, © 1987 Dave Dyer; bottom, courtesy Andy Golovanov. 115: courtesy Andy Golovanov. 116: © 1982 Janeart. 117: © 1985 Frederick Charles, courtesy Manufacturers Hanover. 119: top, © 1985 Janeart; bottom, © 1985 Andrew Popper, Duomo. 120: top, © 1985 Janeart; bottom, © 1982 Tannenbaum, Sygma. 121: © 1985 Adam. J. Stoltman, Duomo.

123: © 1982 Gerard Vandystadt, Agence Vandystadt. 124: © Christian Petit, Agence Vandystadt. 127: © 1982 Gerard Vandystadt, Agence Vandystadt. 129: © 1985 Páll Stefánsson. 131: © 1985 Páll Stefánsson. 132: © 1987 Sandy Treadwell. 133: © 1987 Sandy Treadwell. 134: © 1984 Ricardo Azoury, F4. 135: © 1985 Maier Media. 136, 137: © 1985 Maier Media. 139: © Ricardo Azoury, F4. 140: © 1986 G. Armenise, courtesy Rome Marathon.

143: top, © 1981 Steven E. Sutton, Duomo; bottom, © Steve Powell, All-Sport. 144: courtesy Rome Marathon. 145: courtesy Rome Marathon. 147: © 1985 Sailer/McManus. 149: © 1985 Duomo, Sailer/McManus. 150: © 1985 Duomo, Sailer/McManus. 153: © Kenneth Lee. 155: both, © Kenneth Lee. 157: © 1987 Sandy Treadwell. 158: © Sandy Treadwell. 159: © 1985 Lev Borodulin. 160, 161: © 1985 Lev Borodulin.

162: © Stockholm Marathon. 163: © Stockholm Marathon. 164: © 1987 Sandy Treadwell. 165: © Stockholm Marathon. 167: © Stockholm Marathon. 168: courtesy Vienna Convention Center Hofburg. 169: courtesy Vienna Convention Center Hofburg. 171: courtesy Vienna Convention Center Hofburg.

The Finish
172: © 1984 Tony Duffy, All-Sport. 175: © 1983 Steven E. Sutton, Duomo. 177: © 1985 Trevor Jones, All-Sport. 179: © 1982 Kim Studio. 181: © 1981 Paul J. Sutton, Duomo. 182: © 1979 Takashi Ito. 185: © Simon Miles, All-Sport. 186: © 1984 Trevor Jones, All-Sport.

The type in this book was set in Bodoni Book
on the Mergenthaler Linotron 202
at Trufont Typographers, Hicksville, New York

The book was printed and bound
by Toppan Printing Co., Ltd., Tokyo, Japan